THE STORY
OF THE SHAKERS

The American Shakers

A Celibate, Religious Community

Coeval with the American Republic; First Shaker Family formed at Watervliet, N. Y., 1776 ; First organized Shaker Community established at New Lebanon, N. Y., 1788; Fifteen Shaker Societies in seven States of the United States of America.

Beginnings.

Founder, ANN LEE, of Manchester, England, (1736-1784). In religious revival of 17th Century, arose the "Shaking Quakers," or "Shakers," 1754. Nine persons from Manchester and Bolton, emigrated, May 1774, for the purpose of founding a Shaker Church in America. Eight remained faithful. They were ANN LEE, William Lee, James Whittaker, John Hocknell, James Shepherd, James Partington, Mary Partington, Nancy Lee.

FROM ANN LEE'S TEACHINGS.

Basic Principles of the Shaker Order,

VIRGIN PURITY, PEACE, JUSTICE, LOVE,

expressed in CELIBATE LIFE, NON RESISTANCE, COMMUNITY OF GOODS, UNIVERSAL BROTHERHOOD-- held to be the Divine Order of Society.

Resultant Beliefs and Practices Held as Ideals

TO BE ATTAINED IN THE INDIVIDUAL AND SOCIETY.

Equality of the Sexes, in all departments of life,
Equality in Labor, all working for each, and each for all,
Equality in Property,--No rich, no poor, Industrial Freedom,
  Consecrated Labor, Dedicated Wealth, A United Inheritance,
  Each using according to need,
  Each enjoying according to capacity.
Freedom of Speech, Toleration in Thought and Religion. Often persecuted,
  Shakers have never been known to persecute.
Abolition of all Slavery,--Chattel, Wage, Habit, Passion, Poverty, Disease.
Temperance in all things.
Justice and Kindness to all living beings.
Practical Benevolence. Thou shalt love thy neighbor as thyself.
True Democracy, Real Fraternity, Practical Living of the Golden Rule.

Religious Ideals and Worship.

All life and activity animated by Christian Love is Worship. Shakers adore God as the Almighty Creator, Fountain of all Good, Life, Light, Truth and Love,--the One Eternal Father-Mother.

They recognize the Christ Spirit, the expression of Deity, manifested in fulness in Jesus of Nazareth, also in feminine manifestation through the personality of Ann Lee. Both, they regard as Divine Saviors, anointed Leaders in the New Creation. All in whom the Christ consciousness awakens are Sons and Daughters of God. Spiritual man has, as his divine prerogative and highest destiny, to live in clear conception of and in active harmony with the Highest Good. The Life of the Spirit not the form of expression is essential.

Practical Issues.

Beautiful, comfortable Community Homes, in each a Christ Family.
Daily manual labor for all, according to strength and ability. "Hands to work and hearts to God." (*Ann Lee*)
Opportunity for intellectual and artistic development, within the necessary limits prescribed by the common good.
Sanitation, Health, Longevity.
Simplicity in dress, speech and manner.
Purity in thought, speech and personal habits.
Freedom from debt, worry and competition.

Government.

No Government without God, No Body without a Head.
The Head of the Shaker Order is Christ. The Visible Human Representative is vested in a

DUAL ORDER OF LEADERS.

Spiritual Leaders, of both sexes, a Ministry over Societies, Elders over Families.
Temporal Leaders, of both sexes, Trustees, Deacons and Care-takers, in charge of Business and Industrial Interests.

The Inner Life,

according to the Shaker Faith, is twofold, embracing
  Repentance--confessing and forsaking all sin ;
  Regeneration--the growth and unfoldment in the individual of the Christ Spirit, through living according to the teachings and practice of Jesus Christ. As opposed to the common life of human generation and selfish gratification, this is held to be the Resurrection Life.

Physical development, mental growth and spiritual unfoldment form the only rational basis for a harmonious and happy existence; self-denial the corner-stone of the structure. The truths inherent in Shakerism are the underlying truths of God-life in all ages and the mission of the Shaker is to unfold and demonstrate these truths.

A broadside of Shaker history and belief.

FLO MORSE

The Story
of the Shakers

The Countryman Press
Woodstock, Vermont

Library of Congress Cataloging-in-Publication Data
Morse, Flo.
   The story of the Shakers.
   Reprint of two selections from the author's Yankee communes: The
Shakers : hands to work and hearts to God and the Shakers : the gift of
community. With new foreword and afterword.
   1. Shakers. I. Title.
BX9771.M67 1986   289'.8   85–31430
ISBN 0–88150–062–3 (pbk.)

"Hands to Work and Hearts to God," and "The Gift of Community" reprinted
from *Yankee Communes: Another American Way* by arrangement with the author
and Harcourt Brace Jovanovich, Inc.

Cover: A chair on a pin (peg) is seen through a typical western Shaker arched
doorway in the Centre Family House at Shakertown at Pleasant Hill, Kentucky.
Photograph from *Inner Light: The Shaker Legacy*, by June Sprigg, photographs by
Linda Butler. Photographs Copyright © 1985 by Linda Butler. Reprinted by
permission of Alfred A. Knopf, Inc.

Back cover photo, the Shaker "Tree of Life," courtesy of Ray Pearson

Designed by Robinson Book Associates
Printed in the United States of America
10 9 8 7

*To the memory of Mother Ann Lee
in the 250th anniversary year of her birth
on February 29, 1736*

CONTENTS

Acknowledgments   ix

The Shaker Communities (map)   xii

FOREWORD   *The Shakers: A Religious
Community in an American Tradition*   1

HANDS TO WORK AND HEARTS TO GOD   3

THE GIFT OF COMMUNITY   33

AFTERWORD   *Changes:
The Shakers in the 1980s*   69

WHERE TO FIND SHAKER COLLECTIONS
IN MUSEUMS AND LIBRARIES   93

OTHER BOOKS OF INTEREST   97

FOR FURTHER READING   103

INDEX   105

ACKNOWLEDGMENTS

Sister Ethel Hudson sits on the side of her hospital bed, her legs dangling in warm slippers. At 89, tiny, lightweight, witty, and well except for a skin condition, she is having treatments at the Mary Hitchcock Hospital in Hanover, New Hampshire, far from her East Canterbury, New Hampshire, Shaker home.

She is lonesome for her cat, Buster, who came to her door as a kitten. She shows me his picture.

"He has six toes on each paw," she tells me.

I marvel.

I ask her what she thinks about the future of her Shaker faith.

She says, "I don't think anybody wants to be a Shaker anymore, do you?"

"Yes, I think some do," I say.

I ask if there is anything I can bring her.

With a twinkle, she says, "I love maple walnut ice cream."

I promise to bring some. And she says,

"I'll tend to it right away."

Let me tend to my acknowledgments.

Thank you, Sister Ethel, for our conversations at the hospital. I also thank Eldress Bertha Lindsay and Eldress Gertrude Soule for their time and hospitality, and Richard

Kathmann for his cooperation and information about Shaker Village at Canterbury.

I am very grateful for help on the update of the Shaker story to Brother Ted Johnson, Sister Mildred Barker, Sister Frances Carr, and Brother Arnold Hadd, of Sabbathday Lake, Maine.

Elmer Ray Pearson was generous in providing photographs for the original chapters in *Yankee Communes: Another American Way*. This was the first printing of some of the stereograph views from his archive.

My thanks also to Dr. David Starbuck of Renssalaer Polytechnic Institute; to Walt Chura of the Simple Gifts mission in Albany; to my friend Alfreda Hovey Beck, of Woodstock, Vermont, who grew up among Believers at Mount Lebanon, New York; to Peter Jennison and The Countryman Press, also of Woodstock; to Geneva Menge, librarian of my hometown Lyme Library; and to my husband, Joe, untiring editor-at-home.

I gratefully acknowledge all others who encouraged and aided me in writing this introduction to Shakerism and to the Shakers of yesterday and today.

FLO MORSE
Lyme, New Hampshire

. . . I will shake the heavens and the earth and the sea and the dry land; and I will shake all nations . . . says the Lord of hosts.

—THE OLD TESTAMENT, Haggai 2: 6–7

And all who believed were together and had all things in common; and they sold their possessions and goods and distributed them to all, as any had need. And day by day, attending the temple together and breaking bread in their homes, they partook of food with glad and generous hearts, praising God and having favor with all the people. And the Lord added to their number day by day those who were being saved.

—THE NEW TESTAMENT, Acts 2: 44–47

THE SHAKER COMMUNITIES

1	Watervliet, New York	1787–1938
2	Mount Lebanon, New York	1787–1947
3	Hancock, Massachusetts	1790–1960
4	Harvard, Massachusetts	1791–1918
5	Enfield, Connecticut	1790–1917
6	Tyringham, Massachusetts	1792–1875
7	Alfred, Maine	1793–1932
8	Canterbury, New Hampshire	1792–
9	Enfield, New Hampshire	1793–1923
10	Sabbathday Lake, Maine	1794–
11	Shirley, Massachusetts	1793–1908
12	Gorham, Maine	1808–1819
13	West Union (Busro), Indiana	1810–1827
14	South Union, Kentucky	1807–1922
15	Union Village, Ohio	1806–1912
16	Watervliet, Ohio	1806–1900
17	Pleasant Hill, Kentucky	1806–1910
18	Savoy, Massachusetts	1817–1825
19	Whitewater, Ohio	1824–1916
20	Sodus Bay, New York	1826–1836
21	Groveland, New York	1836–1895
22	North Union, Ohio	1822–1889
23	Narcoossee, Florida	1896–1911
24	White Oak, Georgia	1898–1902

FOREWORD

The Shakers: A Religious Community in an American Tradition

A better world is hard to come by, but that's not for want of trying. Over the ages countless ways to improve society have been tried, and one of the most persistent has been living "in community." In America a native tradition of separate, single-minded communities, following their own way of life, began when the Pilgrims arrived. It blossomed in a golden age of idealistic, utopian communes in the nineteenth century, when the nation was dotted with small, independent communal villages living according to an amazing variety of new social and economic systems.

Among these were religious groups like the Shakers who tried to create heaven on earth. More than most of the reformers, the Shakers succeeded. During the eighteenth century, when they sailed to the New World from England, and the nineteenth, when Shakerism reached its zenith, thousands of men and women, and sometimes entire families, left their homes to live in the Shaker way.

Renouncing marriage and personal property, they lived simply and selflessly in ten states: Kentucky, Ohio, Indiana, New York, Massachusetts, Connecticut, New Hampshire, Maine, Florida and Georgia. While these rural religious retreats were not everyone's idea of utopia, the Shakers were the most successful and are the longest-lasting communitarians in

American history. They gave equal rights to women, welcomed all races, opposed war, strove for perfection in their work, and danced in worship of a Mother-and-Father God.

They still live on in New England. Although greatly reduced in number, members of the United Society of Believers in Christ's Second Appearing keep the faith that asks purity, simplicity and community. And this is a better world for their trying.

F.M.

HANDS TO WORK AND
HEARTS TO GOD

At Manchester, in England,
This blessed fire began,
And like a flame in stubble,
From house to house it ran:
A few at first receiv'd it,
And did their lusts forsake;
And soon their inward power
Brought on a mighty shake.

—"Millennial Praises," 1813

On the ship *Mariah* sailing to America in May, 1774, a small band of nine English emigrants danced and sang. There was such whirling, leaping, trembling, shouting, and rolling on the deck that the captain threatened to throw them overboard. But threats meant nothing to these people. They had been stoned by mobs and flung into jail for disturbing the peace and "profaning the Sabbath" in Manchester, where they came from. This was the way they worshiped. They praised God and felt his power in the strange frenzy that gave them the name of Shakers.

It was in the Manchester prison that their leader, Mother Ann, had received a revelation in a vision. While she was praying in a dark stone cell, she felt the spirit of Christ enter into her. As soon as she was released, she hurried to tell the members of her sect, "Christ dwells within me!"

They could see it in the magnetic new radiance about her. And they marveled that the long-awaited Second Coming of Jesus Christ had happened in a mystical way in the heart of one of their own. Ann Lee had been only a poor ignorant factory girl, whose blue eyes were always seeing visions, before she joined the sect of former Quakers at the age of twenty-two. For nine years she prayed and struggled to deliver her soul from sin, suffering great agony of spirit. And now this simple blacksmith's daughter had become the instrument of God. They whom the English mocked as the "Shaking Quakers" were witnesses to her transformation. To this sect she stood side by side with Jesus, not to be worshiped but as the female manifestation of the spirit of God on earth. Their former leaders, Quaker tailors named James and Jane Wardley, who now stood aside, had led them to expect the Second Coming in the form of a woman. In this they had been influenced by the Camisards, French Protestants who early in the eighteenth century had fled to England for the religious liberty to announce their prophecies and issue their strange warnings.

To the common people of Manchester, however, and of course, to the established Anglican church, all of this was blasphemy, traditionally punished by having a hole burned through the tongue with a red-hot iron. But, brought to trial by church authorities, Mother Ann was spared that fate when she cried out in seventy-two distinct languages. The four ministers who were her judges knew she was unschooled and could not even read or write English. Just in case it was a gift of God, they let her go.

Then the mob took matters into its own hands. If she was not a blasphemer, she was a witch, the angry people decided, and began to pelt her with stones. Curiously, she was untouched, and they backed away as they recognized her supernatural protection, and took to fighting among themselves. Another time it was human aid—an unknown nobleman mysteriously arriving on horseback—that saved her from a threatening mob.

Not long after, when the persecution just as miraculously paused, Mother Ann told the Shakers that those with a "gift" or mind to do so should accompany her to America. "I know God has a chosen people in America," she said. "I saw some of them in a vision and when I meet with them, I will know them."

There was only one member of the little group of Believers in Christ's Second Appearing who had substantial means, and he provided the passage money. And the mission was on its way to carry the good news to the colonies and to establish the Millennial Church in America.

On board the ship with Mother Ann were her elderly benefactor, John Hocknell; her brother, William Lee, a tall handsome blacksmith and former horseman in the royal bodyguard; her niece, Nancy Lee; and a pious young weaver, James Whittaker. The others included Mother Ann's rejected husband, the blacksmith Abraham Stanley. He tagged along hoping Ann would change her mind, but she had already persuaded the Shakers to give up marriage as she had given up hers. To Ann Lee sex was sinful, the root of all trouble, and she thought herself punished for her own sexual experience by the early deaths of all four of her children. And certainly now no personal ties could be allowed to distract the Shakers from their special calling to the service of God.

Their devotion took no rest at sea. When they came up from below loudly singing, dancing, and praying, the nine seemed more like ninety to the captain and his crew. The sailors, tired of being lectured on their wickedness, were ready to throw the Shakers overboard, when suddenly a storm sprang up and all hands were needed on deck. The old sailing vessel began to leak. Even with everyone manning the pumps, the sea poured in so fast the captain feared the ship would sink and all would perish. Mother Ann had faith in God and told him not to worry. "Be of good cheer!" she said. "I see two bright angels standing by the mast, and everything will be all right."

Just as she spoke, a great wave towered over them and struck with violent force. Luckily, it slapped loose timbers into place, which stopped the leak and saved the boat. The Shakers got the credit and the captain gladly carried his peculiar passengers the rest of the three-month voyage to New York.

It was August 6, 1774, one year before the Revolutionary War began, when Mother Ann and her eight followers landed in a strange land and trudged over cobblestoned paths from the New York harbor to Queen Street. They stopped in front of the house of a family named Cunningham, and Mother Ann stepped forward and knocked. When Mrs. Cunningham answered the door, she saw a sturdy woman in her thirties in a long Quaker gray dress with a white kerchief pinned modestly across the top of it. The woman's face was radiant and beautiful in her deep bonnet. The American housewife glanced across the road at two other women with men in strange broad-brimmed hats and long-tailed coats over knee-buckled breeches, then back at Mother Ann, who said, "I have come to preach the gospel to America. An angel of God commanded me to make your house my home." Mrs. Cunningham, so the legend goes, had never seen or heard of the people called Shakers, but she took them in.

Here the wonders ceased. Mother Ann worked for the Cunninghams and others as a laundress. Her husband followed his trade until he became ill and Mother Ann was forced to give up her job to nurse him. They almost starved, but once he was better he left her for a woman of the streets, because Ann still denied him the pleasures of marriage.

The rest of the Shakers had ventured north and were trying to clear a tract of woodland that John Hocknell had leased "in perpetuity" from a Dutch landholder. The old man went back to England for his wife, whose family had earlier had him declared insane for joining the Shakers. But now she returned with him to New York, where they found Mother Ann living in poverty. They brought her up the Hudson River to Niskayuna, the Shakers' first communal home in America, eight miles from Albany.

The year was 1776, and all around there was more and more hostility toward Englishmen. But the Shakers hardly realized it. They had no interest in politics, and like the less emotional Quakers they sprang from, they were opposed to war. They minded their own business, struggling to drain and farm their low swampy land and to build a few log houses.

"Put your hands to work and give your hearts to God," Mother Ann told them. It was her most famous and enduring advice.

TESTIMONIES

OF THE

LIFE, CHARACTER, REVELATIONS AND DOCTRINES

OF

OUR EVER BLESSED MOTHER

ANN LEE,

AND THE ELDERS WITH HER;

THROUGH WHOM THE WORD OF ETERNAL LIFE
WAS OPENED IN THIS DAY OF

CHRIST's SECOND APPEARING:

COLLECTED FROM LIVING WITNESSES,

BY ORDER OF THE MINISTRY,
IN UNION WITH THE CHURCH.

The Lord hath created a new thing in the earth,
A woman shall compass a man.   *JEREMIAH.*

HANCOCK:

PRINTED BY J. TALLCOTT & J. DEMING, JUNRS.

—◦✦◦—

1816.

At the end of each long hard day they still found the energy to worship with the dancing and the shaking they believed rid them of sin and brought them close to God. The time had not yet arrived to spread the word that the Millennium, a thousand years of heaven on earth, had begun. "Wait," said Mother Ann. "They will come like doves."

Patiently the little English group lived in the wilderness at Niskayuna through the signing of the Declaration of Independence and three-and-a-half years of war. They did not attract much attention until the end of a great religious revival at nearby New Lebanon, New York. The revival had attracted hundreds of people from the surrounding border towns of New York and Massachusetts. Such outbursts of religious enthusiasm were common in the colonies, which had experienced a great awakening during the 1730's and 1740's. It was now the middle of the Revolutionary War, and even though only a small number of Americans were actually fighting, wartime brought men to the brink of eternity. Since the established churches offered no comfort or assurance of salvation, anxious men and women in fear of judgment day and damnation for their sins crowded into camp meetings, held in a big barn. They prayed and repented, wept and trembled, fell into trances, saw visions, and finally danced for joy when the revival preachers promised the end of war and sin and the Second Coming of the Lord.

Title page of the so-called "Secret Book of the Elders." The book consisted of a collection of testimonies in defense of Mother Ann, who at one time had been accused of witchcraft, drunkenness, and prostitution. The "Secret Book" was used solely by Shaker elders.

But after the winter nothing came of all the promises, and the hopes and visions faded. Then among the colonists there was talk of a band of holy strangers living together near Albany. It was said they served God day and night and never sinned.

Single seekers and groups—the serious and the curious—went to Niskayuna to see the people called Shakers, who seemed to be expecting them. The visitors stayed for days or weeks, enchanted by Mother Ann and her joyful, melodious songs, her mind reading and body healing and other marvelous gifts. She comforted them by telling them Christ would come again and again in the hearts of the purest people, who confessed their sins, gave up their marriage beds, and righted the wrongs they had committed. One after another, and singly in private interviews rather than in mass conversions, the Americans welcomed the brand-new faith. Husbands and wives often joined at the same time, and sometimes with their whole families.

The original Shakers, who numbered only about a dozen, were kept busy dancing, counseling, cooking, and keeping a clean house for the crowds that came to their door. They were glad to give up their beds and sleep on the floor, and prayed for their own continued strength and guidance.

Eventually the new Believers went home to found little centers of Shakerism in the towns and villages where they lived in New York and New England. Most of them were plain farmers and laborers, many in their early twenties or younger, but among those first converts was Joseph Meacham, a man of forty and a Baptist minister from New Lebanon, New York, who was a leader of the recent revival. His defection to the

Shakers angered the Baptists, who helped spread rumors that the Shakers were really British spies. Why else were these pacifists separating American families and splitting up engaged couples, they asked? Why were they luring people to join them and bring supplies to their colony?

One day in 1780 a young Shaker driving a flock of sheep to Niskayuna was seized by a mob. The sheep were divided, and the youth was carried off to Albany to be tried for treason. Other Shakers who rushed to his defense landed in jail with him when they, too, refused to swear oaths of allegiance or bear arms. Suspected of witchcraft as well as treason, Mother Ann, with her brother and James Whittaker, was arrested and thrown into jail. She pressed her face against the prison bars and preached to crowds that gathered outside about Christ's new kingdom in America. She even made some converts before she was threatened with deportation and sent down the river to Poughkeepsie to be banished behind the enemy's lines.

Many Americans protested the mistreatment of the Shakers by a country fighting for its own freedom and civil rights. And when it was decided that the Shakers were harmless to the new nation's security, and they were all released, they emerged better known than ever.

The following year, 1781, when the American cause looked darkest, Mother Ann and five elders left Niskayuna to visit the scattered converts and strengthen them in the faith. They were on the road for more than two years and covered thirty-six towns and hamlets in Massachusetts and Connecticut. There they tarried in fellow Shakers' homes and taught all who would listen how to "travel" in the way of God.

Hundreds of Yankees were drawn to their singing-dancing meetings, where confession was heard and the spirit of Christ was whispered to be present in the person of Mother Ann Lee.

The Shaker missionaries' home away from home was near Harvard, Massachusetts, and from there they made side trips to nearby villages. Here Mother Ann confronted the people she claimed to have seen before in the vision telling her to go to America. But there were sinister faces in the picture

The "world's people" watch the Shakers worship.

now, for regularly along their route the Shakers met hostile mobs who threatened their lives for breaking up families and churches. Sometimes, outside the houses where they labored or prayed with new Believers, angry crowds gathered with clubs and whips. They broke in the doors and dragged out the defenseless Shakers by their arms and legs and hair and beat the men for blasphemy until their backs bled. Mother Ann would be ordered to show where the English judges burned a hole in her tongue. "Will you believe your own eyes?" she would ask, pulling off her bonnet and sticking out an unblemished tongue. The men would press forward to see. Ashamed when they saw nothing, they would move back, admitting, "They tell awful lies about you."

The Shakers, who practiced the nonviolence as well as the common ownership of the early Christians, were fearless in facing the mobs. But the injuries and brutality they suffered on the mission to New England shortened their lives. They returned safely to Niskayuna in 1783, just as the Peace of Paris was ending the American Revolution. All of them were battered and scarred, and not long after, Mother Ann's brother William Lee died at the age of forty-four. He who had boldly sung, and even composed hymns, at the moment of persecution proved weaker in body than will; his skull had been fractured.

Nor did Mother Ann ever regain her strength. She had premonitions of her own death and spent her last days trying to comfort her followers and the many pilgrims who traveled to see her and were never turned away. "Don't worry!" she reassured them in her cheerful and inspiring way. "You will see peaceable times, and none of the wicked will make you afraid." Like any mother who knows she has to leave her children, she tried to remember everything that could help them carry on without her: how to manage their households with thrift and raise their families in harmony and how to labor faithfully. In words that lived long after her, she told them, "Do all your work as though you had a thousand years to live and as you would if you knew you must die tomorrow."

She urged them to persevere in the way of God and not to heed the lies circulated about her because she preached against lusts of the flesh. But to the pilgrims she said, "Do not go away and report that we forbid to marry: for unless you are able to take up a full cross, and part with every gratification of the flesh, for the Kingdom of God, I would counsel you, and all such, to take wives in a lawful manner, and cleave to them only; and raise up a lawful posterity, and be perpetual servants to your families: for of all lustful gratifications that is the least sin."

In homely sayings that became Shaker law she counseled against laziness, waste, dirt, disorder, and vanity. Finally she foretold the gathering of her disciples into "a united body, or church, having a common interest." But not in her time. She prophesied that American-born Joseph Meacham, now an elder at the Shaker colony at New Lebanon, would be the one to do the gathering. Her blue eyes peered into the future as she predicted, "The next opening of the gospel will be in the Southwest. It will be at a great distance, and there will be a great work of God."

Just before she died in 1784, a year after her return from the missionary journey, Mother Ann had a vision in which Brother William came in a golden chariot to take her home. And John Hocknell, an old man, but still gifted in visions, insisted that he saw her soul wafted heavenward in just such a chariot, drawn by four white horses. Mother Ann was only forty-eight at her death, but her work on earth was done.

Already the "chosen people in America" far outnumbered the few who had come to the New World to save them. To these American Shakers, Mother Ann was immortal. They did not falter long, and the strong did not "fall away" from the faith when she left them. Her successor was thirty-three-year-old James Whittaker, who as a little boy was said to have kept her alive in an English jail, where she was left to starve, by feeding her milk and wine through a pipe passed through a keyhole.

Father James, an inspired preacher whose zeal was second only to Mother Ann's, began to prepare the Shakers for the next step—separating from the hostile and sinful world. They would have to leave their homes and make a life together for protection and security against persecution. This would mean breaking off natural family ties completely and would be especially hard on young members who joined the sect over the objections of skeptical parents and husbands and wives. Strong leaders would be needed for such a transition, and, seeking them, Father James tried to visit every place Shakers lived, even as far away as Maine and New Hampshire. Some had already set up communal living in the homes of well-to-do members. But those still isolated in their own homes were cautioned by Father James against the world's corruptions. "I warn you, brethren," he said, "not to be overcome with the cares of this world, lest your souls lose the power of God and you become lean and barren." He even disapproved of Shakers in western Massachusetts taking sides on issues like Shays' Rebellion, when poor desperate farmers armed with staves and pitchforks marched against the state.

When he dedicated the first meetinghouse at New Lebanon in 1786, Father James introduced the new "gospel orders" and the kind of discipline the Shakers would eventually live by. "Ye shall come in and go out of this house with reverence and godly fear," he announced. "All men shall come in and go out at the west doors and gates; and all women at the east doors and gates. Men and women shall not intermix in this house or yard, nor sit together; neither shall there be any whispering or talking or laughing or unnecessary going out and in, in times of public worship."

The last of the English Shaker ministers of Christ, Father James wore himself out by his long journeys and his effort to hold the Believers together. Ill health forced him to retire to Enfield, Connecticut, leaving Joseph Meacham in charge of the home church at New Lebanon. And when Father James died in 1787, Father Joseph completed his work of separating the Shakers from the world. As Mother Ann had predicted, it fell to this less saintly and more practical man, their first American leader, to organize the Shakers into a series of independent village-communes, a United Society of Believers in Christ's Second Appearing.

Father Joseph chose a woman, Sister Lucy Wright of Pittsfield, Massachusetts, to be the "leading character in the female line" and set the pattern for a dual order of government with equality of the sexes far in advance of the times. Lucy had been only twenty-seven when, keeping her maiden name, she followed her husband Elizur Goodrich into the Shaker ranks to live as a single woman. Mother Ann was so impressed with her that she called her joining "equal to gaining a nation." Not only was Lucy handsome, forceful, and intelligent, but she came from a good Providence, Rhode Island, family and lent prestige to the Shakers.

Father Joseph and Mother Lucy made their headquarters at New Lebanon, and the New York community became the mother church. It was the first to collect its members into the way of life the Shakers called "society-order." Next to do so was Niskayuna (later called Watervliet), where Mother Ann lay buried in a humble grave. A decade after her death there were ten other Shaker communes in New England, patterned on New Lebanon, at Harvard, Hancock, Tyringham, and Shirley in Massachusetts; Enfield in Connecticut; Canterbury and Enfield in New Hampshire; and Gorham, Alfred, and New Gloucester (later Sabbathday Lake) in Maine.

So many came together in those early years that there were high hopes of saving the world. The challenge rang out:

Hats and broom hang outside brethren's rooms.

"Make room for thousands!" Everyone suffered and sacri-
ficed to expand the kingdom of God for all who wanted to
join it. Big communal dwellings were prepared, and the New
Hampshire man who framed the first meetinghouse was in
great demand. For eight or nine years Brother Moses Johnson
traveled from group to group building ten more plain churches
without spires—not "the devil's steeple-houses" that Mother
Ann had disliked. He also raised barns, hogsties, and gristmills,
leaving his stamp on Shaker architecture, before he slid back
into the "common course" of the world, not the first or the
last of the Shakers to do so.

Bonnets, cloaks, and broom at entrance to sisters' rooms.

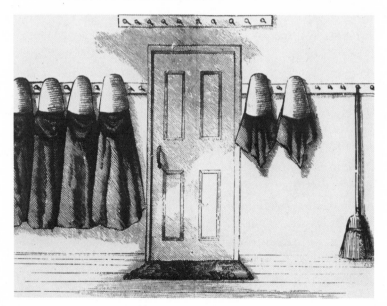

Most of the communities grew around estates of stauncher members like Benjamin Whitcher of Canterbury, who had kept a houseful of New Hampshire Shakers for ten years. But it was not only large donations of land and labor that helped establish the new colonies; incoming Shakers made many smaller contributions. As they wound up their affairs, paid off their debts, and withdrew from the world, they brought into the fold all kinds of possessions—livestock and wagons, beds and bedding, grain and feed and household goods. It was not only inspirational, but practical and necessary to follow the example of the first Christians, who "had all things common."

Aiming to be as pure and chaste as they had been, the Shakers separated husbands and wives. Their children were placed in separate orders for girls and boys, where they were no longer the special concern of their parents. They all became part of the extended families that made up each Shaker commune. Every family was governed by a set of elders and eldresses, deacons and deaconesses, and trustees, male and female, who handled the spiritual, social, and business affairs of its thirty- to ninety-odd members.

There were usually three families in a society. New Lebanon at one time included eight families. They were either numbered as they were gathered, or named geographically— Center Family, South Family, Hill Family, and so on.

The central ministry skillfully guided and unified the new way of life, dispatching elders where needed to help the new sisters and brethren adjust and conform. And in the matching societies where men and women were equal and obedient, each sex dressed uniformly and lived at arm's length

Silent meals at separate tables.

from each other. Before long there was "gospel order." This differed from the world's order not only in joint ownership of goods, but in the strict separation of the sexes. Sisters and brethren were forbidden to pass on the stairs, to enter each other's rooms or place of work, to give or receive presents, or ever to touch each other. To safeguard these arrangements and many other social regulations, separate staircases were built wherever possible, separate workshops were maintained, narrow paths and separate doors were used. Also, there were separate dining tables at the common meals eaten in monastic silence.

A daily disciplined round of work and worship honored Mother Ann's major principle of "hands to work and hearts to God." Work was done with care, as Mother Ann had ordered.

The Shakers had begun trades and handcrafts even before the communes were organized, and now their trustees handled sales of garden seeds and medicinal herbs and farm produce to the world. Only trustees dealt with outsiders, who gradually learned to respect the creativity of Shaker hands and to trust the honesty of Shaker hearts. Brethren in broad-brimmed hats went out on the road in America's first one-horse wagons to peddle "things Shaker" to a growing market.

While their occupations were rewarding and profitable, worship was the Shakers' chief joy and recreation. Now that they lived in groups, their dancing meetings were family-style. When Mother Ann had passed like an inspiration among them, they had danced individually to her cry, "Be joyful, brethren and sisters! Be joyful! Joy away! Rejoice in the God of your salvation!" Now there were no more impulsive whirlings, no wandering off alone in a trance, as in her day, after one's own outstretched arm. Instead, everyone memorized the sacred shuffling steps revealed to Father Joseph in a vision of the angels marching and countermarching and circling the throne of God. Not a dancing man, but an intensely spiritual and conscientious one, he practiced the steps alone in his room before teaching them to the Believers.

From Mother Lucy the dancers learned to hold their hands aloft cupped in the ancient prayerful way to receive God's love, and to shake their hands down to release evil. Dancing, rehearsed and structured, with the brethren lined up on one side and the sisters on the other, became an impressive ritual, like Shaker life itself. Later, it became an exhibition, sometimes with 300 or 400 Shakers participating and the "world's people" watching from the sidelines.

When the disciples of Mother Ann were safely within tidy well-run collectives, Father Joseph died suddenly in 1796, exhausted from constant travel and effort. His great work of organization was done: all Shakers had left the world, renounced the flesh, confessed their sins and contributed their property to the church. A simple verbal covenant, all that had bound them until a year before his death, had been put into writing. The way of life "wherein they were called to travel" was making spiritual and practical progress when, for the first time in years, there came an outside diversion.

Mother Lucy was supreme head of the ministry when news reached New Lebanon of a strong religious awakening on the distant frontiers of Ohio, Kentucky, and Tennessee. She was reminded at once of Mother Ann's prophecy and decided to "open the gospel in the Southwest," where the great Kentucky Revival was already in its fifth year.

It had erupted out of a series of camp meetings sponsored by the Presbyterians to stimulate religion on the frontier. But instead of benefiting the established churches, new sects had sprung up. They dispensed with clergymen and creeds and offered revelations and salvation direct from God. The Shakers, who had developed into a full-fledged sect after the New Lebanon Revival, now saw a chance to harvest western souls and grew excited at the possibility of sending missionaries to the frontier.

Early on New Year's Day, 1805, three men from the New Lebanon Community, their baggage loaded on a single horse, set out on foot on a 1,200-mile trip over wilderness trails to Kentucky. Issachar Bates was a Revolutionary War veteran who had fathered eleven children before he joined the Shakers.

Kitchen sisters share their work. "See that your victuals are prepared in good order and on time, so that when the brethren return from their labors in the fields they can bless you and eat their food with thankfulness."

John Meacham was Father Joseph's son. And Benjamin Seth Youngs was a Shaker scholar. They would make good missionaries.

Their path across the country led through New York, Philadelphia, Baltimore, Washington, and then over the Appalachian Mountains. Two months and twenty-two days after they left home they found the "first rest for the soles of their feet" in a simple log cabin in Turtle Creek, Ohio. There, a frontiersman named Malcolm Worley and his wife listened eagerly as the Shakers warmed themselves before the fire. The midwesterners were excited to hear about the new communal way of life and religion. That very night they accepted the faith and confessed their sins to these dynamic men of God, so filled with hope and courage. "All that I have is yours!" promised Malcolm Worley, gripping the hands of the three men. His property became the first Shaker communal holding in the West. Within a few weeks more families joined their small group and added their land and goods.

The most important convert was the Worleys' pastor, Richard McNemar, an educated Presbyterian minister of a reformed or New Light Church. He had been one of the founders of the Kentucky Revival movement, but was forced to watch it grow out of control like a prairie fire and go to extremes.

He told the Shakers how the God-driven people, massed together in the forest, turned from sin to the Lord. Inflamed night and day by the holy spirit, hungry for righteousness and sinlessness, many responded hysterically, screaming in their anguish, barking like dogs, jerking without stopping, baying on all fours, rolling like logs, falling down stiff as corpses.

Community at South Union, Kentucky. A black family of ex-slaves was part of the Shaker community at South Union after the Civil War. Black Shakers lived with white members in many northern societies.

Nonetheless, this enthusiastic revival atmosphere favored the work of the Shaker missionaries. With the minister on their side, and with preaching and singing, they won his entire flock and competed successfully with the old churches and the new sects for the saved. "Here was a people waiting for us," wrote Issachar Bates from the West. "They were very swift to hear and confess their sins, and we left them rejoicing." New Shaker societies were born, and Brother Issachar walked all the way back to New Lebanon for money to buy land to settle them on. In fact, in ten years' time he traveled 38,000 miles, mostly on foot, and listened to the private con-

fessions of more than a thousand new Believers in Christ's Second Appearing.

Among the eastern Shakers, the excitement in the Southwest gave rise to a sympathetic revival and a boost to the faith. Sisters and brethren followed Brother Issachar back to help organize communal homes for "Mother's children" in the West, at South Union and Pleasant Hill in Kentucky, and Union Village and Watervliet in Ohio. Later "there was a gift," as the Shakers put it, to establish colonies at Whitewater, Ohio, and North Union (Shaker Heights) near Cleveland. The westernmost colony, founded at Busro, Indiana, suffered

continually from malaria, Indian raids, and the brutal occupa-
tion of soldiers, and its members had to move in wagons and
flatboats to join the other groups.

Indians were the least of the western Shakers' problems.
All the religious prejudice, persecution, and violence of New
England were repeated, with the added lawlessness of the
frontier mob. Issachar Bates recorded on his journey to Indiana in 1808:

> . . . They came upon us on horseback with ropes to
> bind us, headed by one John Thompson. He stepped up
> to me and said "Come prepare yourselves to move."
> "Move where," says I. "Out of this country," said
> he, "for you have ruined a fine neighborhood, and now
> we intend to fix you. Your hats are too big, we shall
> have a part of them off, and your coats are too long,
> we shall have a part of them off. And seeing you will
> have nothing to do with women, we will fix you so that
> you will not be able to perform. . . ."

Fortunately, the Governor of the Indiana Territory intervened
and saved them.

As time passed, the Believers in the West, as in the East,
were accepted as good farmers and neighbors. Legend has it
that one town in Ohio declined as a result of persecuting the
Shakers and another prospered because its citizens treated
them kindly. Slowly the western settlements grew in land
holdings and became strong in leadership and influence. They
all shared in a social system that segregated the sexes while it
united the labor of their hands and hearts.

Before the middle of the nineteenth century there were
eighteen sturdy Shaker societies, subdivided into fifty-eight

family units. On vast and rolling farms, spreading from Maine almost to the Mississippi, 6,000 thrifty Shakers worked toward perfection. They were certain God's kingdom had come and they were living in it, unmarried, and unsullied as angels. They were also proud of the religious communism adopted in their withdrawal from the world. They were the first Yankee —native-born—communists, having inherited the religion and

Intercommunity visits were rare in winter, but Shakers enjoyed their sleigh rides.

way of life followed by one of the earliest immigrant communal sects.

By this time the Shakers—the United Society of Believers in Christ's Second Appearing—offered the best model of the good life possible in small, planned communities. The system of sexual and social equality that was part of their religion was studied and envied by other less successful reformers. By the 1840's there were many nonreligious community hopefuls, as there had been in the 1820's with the inspiration and example of Robert Owen at New Harmony in Indiana. Among them were the New England transcendentalists' Brook Farm, where Nathaniel Hawthorne and an intellectual company milked cows and shared farm chores. Later he wrote satirically about that utopian community in *The Blithedale Romance*. Fruitlands was a short-lived dream of Louisa May Alcott's father, Bronson Alcott, who refused to let his vegetarian communal family even use animals for field work because he considered it slave labor. There was also a legion of phalanxes, profit-sharing associations based on agriculture and industry and a system of labor "groups" and "series." In the farming series were plowing groups, haying groups, planting groups, and milking groups, and in the industrial series, carpenters' groups, shoemakers' groups, and so on. The least attractive work earned the highest wage of ten cents an hour, in these popular American attempts to achieve the fantastic reorganization of society proposed by an eccentric French socialist writer, Charles Fourier.

Even if the more practical Shakerdom was not everyone's idea of utopia, it had become a national curiosity before mid-century. The sober hard-working society that nonetheless danced in its churches won a lot of attention from the general public to whom it had made familiar the idea of people living communally.

During the American Revolution Mother Ann had told her children, "Wait, they will come like doves." And looking for closer and more reassuring religious experience, pilgrims had found their way to the people called Shakers.

The United Society always had high hopes of conversions. On the Sabbath they opened wide the special entrances in the meetinghouses for the "world's people," and inside they set up bleachers. Americans and foreign tourists flocked to the spectacle of the sisters and brethren shuffling and shaking away their sin.

This popular song, recorded here in Shaker notation, came by inspiration in 1848 to Elder Joseph Brackett at Alfred, Maine.

THE GIFT OF COMMUNITY

'Tis the gift to be simple, 'tis the gift to be free,
'Tis the gift to come down where we ought to be.
And when we find ourselves in the place just right,
'Twill be in the valley of love and delight.
When true simplicity is gain'd,
To bow and to bend we shan't be ashamed,
To turn, turn will be our delight
Till by turning, turning, we come round right.

—"Simple Gifts," *revival song, received by inspiration*

In 1843 a celebrated visitor from abroad journeyed to New Lebanon, New York, headquarters of the Shaker church. As he approached the quiet village, he passed a crew of Shakers working on the road and thought them "very wooden men as if they had been so many figure-heads of ships." His carriage continued to the beginning of the village, and at the door of a building where the Shakers sold their wares, he requested permission to see the Shaker worship.

Of all people, Charles Dickens, concluding his American tour, was turned away. He took revenge in his book *American Notes*, in which he described his short visit to the Shakers:

"We walked into a grim room, where several grim hats were hanging on grim pegs, and the time was grimly told by a grim clock which uttered every tick with a kind of struggle, as if it broke the grim silence reluctantly and under protest. Ranged against the wall were six or eight stiff high-backed chairs and they partook so strongly of the general grimness, that one would much rather have sat on the floor than incurred the smallest obligation to any of them.

"Presently there stalked into this apartment a grim old Shaker, with eyes as hard and dull and cold as the great round buttons on his coat and waistcoat: a kind of calm goblin. Being informed of our desire, he produced a newspaper wherein the body of elders, whereof he was a member, had advertised but a few days before that in consquence of certain unseemly interruptions which their worship had received from strangers, their chapel was closed to the public for the space of one year."

No exceptions could be made. Whereupon Dickens left and later wrote from hearsay all the unpleasant things about the Shakers he could remember.

The elder meant no offense. The Shakers were entirely occupied with a mysterious influence that had invaded their domain. The "world's people" could not be expected to understand it.

This influence began one day in 1837 when several teen-age sisters at Watervliet, New York, suddenly began to tremble and felt compelled to whirl around their classroom without stopping until they fell into a faint. After they came to, they had greetings from the "spirit land" and tales of a heavenly trip. Other children were affected, and before long adults had seizures, too. The phenomenon traveled from east to west. For the next ten years and longer all the Shaker communes were flooded with spiritual messages, songs and dances seen in visions, inspired drawings, prophecies, and even new book-length revelations of God's will. It was a new high in spirit power, even for the Shakers, to whom spiritualism was nothing new. Their whole history was remarkable. The faith had begun with a vision in an English jail and reached America with the help of two angels at sea. Unusual powers had marked the missionary work of foundress Mother Ann Lee and her few followers. Their strange wordless songs and dancing seemed part of an abundance of supernatural gifts and godsends.

And now among those who never knew her, there had come this remarkable increase in inspiration, which the central ministry solemnly declared to be "Mother Ann's work." And with it the four leading elders and eldresses saw a chance to purge the church of a certain worldliness and vanity that had crept in with material success. They told the Shakers in all the communes that Mother Ann wanted her children to return to the purity and plainness of her time.

And lo! there came divine commands for cleaning house and confessing sin and holding mysterious ceremonies on sacred grounds. At night the Shakers were roused for prayer and marched through their buildings with imaginary spiritual brooms. By day they swept the floors with the actual flat broom they had invented. They scrubbed the brethren's, sisters' and children's workshops with sand, cleared every barn, pen, and field of litter and rubbish, until the communes renowned in America for their neatness were tidier than ever before.

As they labored for the gift to be simple, the Shakers played childlike games. They threw themselves into fantasy and dramatics, and were anything but "grim." "Only a Dickens," someone said, "could describe their antics."

Dickens would have delighted in what went on behind closed doors. But large white wooden crosses kept the public away. The world's people were not thought to be ready for psychic phenomena and would only ridicule or fear it. Meanwhile, business continued as usual during the spiritual alterations—dealings in packaged seeds and herbs, brushes and brooms, chairs and oval wooden boxes, sold with the Shakers' famous trademark of honesty and good measure.

Sacred Shaker dance at a secret mountain meeting.

Who had time for the courteous reception of outsiders, when the great of all ages were dropping in? Noah, Alexander, Napoleon and his generals, Queen Esther and George Washington, to name a few, were visualized by the Shakers, to whom the departed were as real an influence as the living.

Even Jesus was reported to be dwelling among the Shakers in this period. In 1843, while thousands of followers of the Reverend William Miller, who predicted the end of the world, waited on roofs and mountain tops for the Second Coming, Shakers in Ohio complacently claimed Jesus was with them at North Union. When the world did not end as expected, some of the disappointed Millerites went insane, and some committed suicide. Some went home and picked up their old lives. Many joined the Shakers, who believed the Millennium had already arrived.

These newcomers, and others from communal sects that foundered, were always welcomed by the Believers. And welcome, too, during this revival, were the wandering spirits of pagans—Africans, Orientals, Indians, and Eskimos—who came seeking salvation. That the dead could still be converted to find eternal rest in heaven was a belief of the Shakers of those times. To them, heaven was a Shaker community on a large scale, where Jesus and Mother Ann were head elder and eldress. Both the Son and the Daughter of God kept in close touch with Shakerdom, the eighteen heavenly societies below. At this time Mother Ann sent frequent messages through members who were called mediums or instruments. Once at a meeting in Watervliet, New York, a sister whirled around in one place for fifteen minutes without stopping or becoming dizzy. Then she ran and whispered her message to the eldress, who gave her permission to announce, "A tribe of savage Indians has been around two days. They're outside the building now, looking in the windows! Mother Ann says to take in the poor spirits and assist them to get salvation!"

Only a new convert might look fearfully toward the windows. But the others entered into the game. The doors were thrown open, and the sister who could "see" the Indians invited them to come in. At once the Shakers became "possessed" of the spirits of squaws and braves. They squatted on the floor together in Indian style, while the elders and eldresses tried to keep them apart in Shaker style. A regular powwow took place, with whooping and yelling and singsong, before the Indians were considered saved and the sisters and brethren returned to their normally dignified selves.

Many Shakers had to labor for "the eye of faith" in order to share the "visitations" and spiritual fun and see the presents Mother Ann sent her children—samples of what waited in God's country for a faithful Shaker who denied his flesh on earth. There was heavenly wine from her celestial vineyard, which made the Believers drunk; glorious crowns and robes they dressed up in; caskets of treasure they divided; baskets of fruit they devoured; and musical instruments they tooted and plucked as they marched around in a parade. A special shipment of spiritual guns arrived for the brethren from George Washington.

Under the influence of spirits, the Shakers sang, "Come, come, who will be a fool?"—and each in an effort to be humble would answer, "*I* will be a fool!" They shared the laughing gift, lodged by a spirit in a medium without a sense of humor. Fortunately, the gift was contagious and traveled around at a

After whirling like a top, a Shaker medium falls into a faint.

meeting until everyone rocked in his straight-backed chair, or even rolled on the floor.

Excitement simmered beneath the outward calm of each Shaker communal village. No one knew who would become an instrument next, seized by the spirit and personality of someone who had departed from this life. A sister or brother could be struck down to the floor and struggle as if with a demon, or else be set spinning like a top, or rush back and forth as if driven by the wind. Sometimes the mediums fell into a swoon and remained in a trance for hours or even days, while the family tiptoed around them, eager for their first words or notes.

Nothing seen or heard in vision was ever rejected by the democratic Shakers. Each gift of song—no matter if there were thousands—was prized and recorded in the peculiar musical notation given to Mother Ann by inspiration. There was some warning about "overstepping the real gift" and pretending to be God's Holy Anointed One when one was not. Occasionally, false spirits were discovered through the spiritual "spectacles" or insights of the elders, who listened to all messages first and were not beyond using a medium to expose sin.

Most of the inspiration, however, flowed in and out of pure hearts. Sometimes a sensitive person "in the gift" was excused from his or her normal duties to retire to a quiet place, returning with twenty or more songs in a single day. It was a gift in itself for the Shakers to be able to sing some of the songs, since many mediums spoke in unknown tongues, and to dance in authentic native fashion with the pagan spirits.

Moreover, the Believers who were moved to draw or paint their heavenly visions had never been artists before. The Shakers disapproved of pictures and hung none on their walls. They were counted among the vanities of the world, like ornate clocks, looking-glasses and bureaus, and odd or fanciful architecture. Usefulness was the sole criterion in their own built-in cupboards and functional furniture and in their massive family dwellings, shops, and barns. And if in the creation of utility they produced a singular beauty, it was incidental. "Let it be plain and simple," went a Shaker tenet, "of good and substantial quality, unembellished by any super-fluities which add nothing to its goodness or durability."

Completely contrary to "Shaker order" were the spirit or inspirational drawings. They were full of forbidden, worldly, and probably longed-for ornaments, quaint symbols, and small cramped verses and blessings in neat spidery script. Drawn with joyful flourishes, though not abandon, were wings of freedom, swords of power, trumpets of wisdom, crowns of glory, doves of love, birds of paradise, tempered by cups of humility. Colors like red, ordinarily considered immodest, were used. But who could refuse a Valentine from a vanished hand, probably female, because it was delivered in red ink?

"I received a draft of a beautiful tree," wrote inspired Sister Hannah Cahoon from the "City of Peace" (Hancock, Massachusetts), "pencilled on a large sheet of white paper bearing ripe fruit. I saw it plainly. It looked singular curious to me. I have since learned that this tree grows in the spirit land. Afterward, the spirit showed me plainly the branches, leaves and fruit painted or drawn upon paper. The leaves were checked or crossed and the same colors. I entreated Mother Ann to tell me the name of this tree, which she did Oct. 1st, 4 hour p.m. by moving the hand of a medium to write twice over, 'Your tree is the tree of life.' "

It was a favorite Shaker symbol. Father James Whittaker had seen a burning vision of such a tree before he set out with Mother Ann to establish the Millennial Church in America.

By the mid-1840's the Shakers had given good measure to a "swift-winged" Holy Angel, who had demanded, "More zeal, more life, more fervency, more energy, more love, more thankfulness, more obedience, more strength, more power!" Within the next few years, they stopped trailing home exhausted from semiannual pilgrimages to the "feast grounds" that each community had been ordered to set aside and enclose. On these holy mounts and sacred plains they had sown spiritual seed, washed in spiritual fountains, and danced in the early "promiscuous" style, each Shaker for himself. Gradually, the communities ended most of the rituals required during the era of Mother's Work and closeted the spiritual brooms.

The Tree of Life in this inspired, or "spirit," drawing is a symbol of the Shaker church.

Fewer and fewer messages were divinely posted, although inspiration remained a Shaker gift.

Some thoughtful Believers had been put off by what seemed child's play. Others were proud of the imaginative resources unleashed. Among these were two major revelations. One had a mouth-filling title—"A Holy, Sacred and Divine Roll and Book from the Lord God of Heaven to the Inhabitants of Earth"—and 500 copies were proudly dispatched to the rulers of the world. Later it was discredited. The only one who took it seriously enough to say thank you was the King of Sweden and Norway.

The other king-sized manuscript was a Shaker seeress's defense of extrasensory perception and the possibility of God's continuing to express his will. Why not consider God's revelations a growing thing, like natural science, she asked, instead of something delivered once and for all time?

The worst result of the spiritualist revival was the loss of the outstanding member of the western groups. After thirty-four years as a leader, Richard McNemar was expelled from the order when a medium falsely denounced him to a jealous elder. At the age of sixty-nine, he was given only his clothes and his printing press to enable him to earn a living elsewhere. When the ministry in the East learned what had befallen him, McNemar was reinstated. But by that time he had grown ill and soon died.

No wonder Mother Ann was heard by a medium to grumble, "I foresee the evil of my word being too plenty among the people." The spirits who dwelled among the Shakers announced their own departure and went off, according to the Believers, to manifest themselves to the world. The United

Society waited. And sure enough, in 1848, a strange influence began to stir among the "world's people." It started with young girls, just as it had among the Shakers.

Two farmer's daughters in Rochester, New York, began to communicate with a mysterious spirit who rapped on the walls of their house at night. "Here, Mr. Splitfoot," taunted one of the girls, referring to the cloven foot of the devil, "do as I do!" She tapped—and the spirit tapped back.

The Shakers insisted that their spirits had produced the Rochester rappings. They were very much interested in the exchange, which became so famous that the girls performed it before great crowds in public lecture halls. Even though it later turned out that they were just cracking their joints, Katie and Maggie Fox—and not the genuinely inspired Shakers—got the credit for the birth of modern spiritualism in America.

Though the Shakers considered the new American spiritualism theatrical, they themselves were onstage once a week. The Sabbath meetings were reopened to the public, and many people came to see the show. Some spectators even contributed money to the Shakers in return for the entertainment they received.

If the sisters and brethren felt self-conscious in front of an audience of "world's people," it was not for long. Moving from half-circles at each end of the room, the men on one side and the women on the other, with the singers in the middle, they were soon swept up in the joy of the sacrament. Onlookers shared the thrill of the quick-footed worshipers, who danced in a throng in perfect rhythm with symbolic gestures of their hands.

Shakers worship in the dance, hands cupped to receive God's love.

More than anything else, the dance communicated the kind of joy and freedom there was in being a Shaker—freedom from the evils and pressures of the world, freedom from the burden of sins of the flesh. The purity and virginity of which they were so proud were reflected in the sisters' Sunday gowns of white, with white caps, blue aprons and blue pointed, high-heeled shoes, and the brethren's long-tailed blue coats and trousers. Before long the coats were discarded and the men danced in their shirtsleeves—and never touched the women.

A singing meeting brings sisters and brethren face to face.

For this performance there were rehearsals during the week, and new songs and dances were practiced. At evening social meetings, six or eight brethren sat in a row of straight chairs facing a row of sisters four feet away. There was conversation as well as singing, and it was a more congenial grouping than it looked.

Sometimes sitting opposite the brethren were the sisters who took care of their household and wardrobe needs. The women sewed their buttons and made their beds in the morning after the men left the room and all bedding had been hygienically aired. This natural social arrangement was one that caused malicious gossip outside the communes. The virtuous folk who shook themselves free of sinful thoughts were never able to shake off the slander of a deserted husband or wife whose mate had joined them, or the exposés of those who "fell back" into the world. Shaker celibacy, with men and women living on the same floor in the same household, stirred the public's imagination and indignation. Throughout the nineteenth century many detailed accusations and many suggestive descriptions of short stays among the Shakers were read as eagerly as novels.

Gossip also accused women of signing the covenant to lure away one of the brethren for a husband. One sister did run off with no less than a New Hampshire elder. But for the few exceptions there were hundreds more who embraced Shakerism as a refuge from marriage or the need to marry for economic and social security. Long before women's liberation movements, the Shakers guaranteed the rights of women and gave them every opportunity to progress, or travel. A line of notable women reached the position of eldress, where they were completely equal with elders in governing.

The Shakers' material comforts and social advantages were much admired. Some observers thought even a man could do no wiser thing than join them. Many a "winter Shaker" put up with what he privately considered ridiculous ceremonies for a good warm home until spring.

Despite large numbers of transients, freeloaders, and backsliders, the Shaker societies reached peak membership and prosperity in the decade before the Civil War. This was the golden age in the peace-loving hamlets, where paint never peeled from the buildings and the crystal windows reflected heaven. Nothing was "foul or noisy" along the neat avenues, and when the poet Walt Whitman came to visit, even the dust in the road seemed pure to him.

Daily, at specific hours, the inhabitants rose, prayed, ate, labored, held meetings, and retired. No one was overworked, and there was a wide variety of occupations. Shakers took great pleasure in improving their skills and mastering several trades. Everyone worked, including the elders and eldresses in the special ministry shops. It was almost natural that out of such industry—so many "hands to work"—there would be a flow of invention, an outpouring of mechanical gifts.

The list is long of things the Shakers made first or made better: among them, the common clothespin, cut nails, the flat broom, the circular saw, a metal pen, a rotary harrow, a tongue-and-groove machine, a screw propeller, a threshing machine, an improved washing machine, a pea sheller, an apple parer, a revolving oven, and an improved wood-burning stove. They also made water-repellent cloth and combination window sash.

Hundreds of additional time savers, shortcuts, gadgets, and plans for organizing huge building and irrigation projects were traded like songs and recipes among the fifty-eight energetic families in the chain of Shaker societies across the nation. Sometimes an outsider took advantage of their groundwork in research. The vacuum vessel that Gail Borden borrowed and used for several months among the Shakers at New Lebanon led to his profitable invention of condensed milk.

For a long time the Shakers had no trouble keeping down on such creative farms the many young people, or-

Shaker children.

phans, and unwanted children they took in from the world.
There were no public institutions for their care. The Shakers'
charity was in part self-interest, a source of future members
needed for the survival of the faith. Some societies preferred
even bad children to none, while others would adopt only
those who came with their parents, often widowed mothers
seeking a safe haven, or children left with them by a widowed
father. Whenever there were national and local epidemics and
disasters, the Shakers sent generous amounts of money and
wagonfuls of food and clothing to victims, in addition to offer-
ing shelter to orphans.

The children were brought up, educated, and taught a trade or useful arts by members who were devoted to them. In the children's order they lived regulated, happy lives, with many companions and dedicated caretakers. Like their older sisters and brethren, they were expected to keep step, follow the lead and march together toward heaven and life eternal. "The Youth's Guide in Zion" instructed: "Never try to run on ahead before the main body of good believers, and above all, never fall back; but keep up close and be in the gift."

But how did one obey the elders and "the gift" at the same time? A boy who lived with the Shakers was asked whether he could do as he pleased.

"Of course," replied the youth, "We can do whatever we have the gift to."

If he wanted to go ice skating on a winter morning, what would he do?

"I would tell the elder that I had a gift to go down and skate."

Would the elder let him go?

"Certainly," said the boy, "unless the elder had a gift that I should not go."

But if he told the elder that he had a gift to go down and skate and he must go . . . ?

"Why, then," said the boy, "the elder would tell me that I had a 'lying gift' and *he* had a gift to beat me if I did not go about my work at once!"

Corporal punishment was actually rare. In its place, Mother Ann's advice for raising children was applied. She did not believe that children inherited "original sin." "Little children," she said, "are nearer the kingdom of Heaven than

Two young Shakers at Canterbury, New Hampshire, where Shaker boys had their own small farm.

those who have grown to riper years. They are simple and innocent, and if they were brought up in simplicity, they would receive good as easily as they would evil." Partial to young people, she warned parents, "Do not speak to children in a passion, or you will put devils into them. Do not cross them unnecessarily, for it makes them ill-natured, and little children do not know how to govern their nature."

As the young Shakers grew older in the company of consecrated workers, they took their place in the households and shops and gardens that were extensions of the church. They learned to do all their work in Mother's way—as if they had a thousand years to live and as they would do it if they were to die the next day. They learned from the seedsmen how to grow and select the garden seeds that Shakers were the first to package and which they had been selling since 1790.

At New Lebanon they built slat-back chairs, rocking chairs, chairs that tilted back on a ball in a socket, and some that even swiveled. They gathered and cultivated wild medicinal herbs and roots—bugle, belladonna, burdock, horehound, sweetfern, wintergreen—for the extracts, salves, and syrups that were Shaker remedies, as well as for use in the medicines made by "the world."

In the tall brick dwellings the girls cleaned the rooms well, having been taught that "good spirits will not live where there is dirt." They hung chairs and garments on the high peg boards that lined every Shaker room, and swept the floor beneath them. In the fragrant kitchen they prepared wholesome food, and in the common dining room none of it was wasted.

Later many of the skilled young farmers, artisans, and

housekeepers marched off—to tunes more exciting than gift songs—to factories and cities. Few of the children raised by the Shakers—only one or two in ten—remained to sign the covenant that gave their lives to God. Countless youths, however, carried away lifetime habits of neatness, thrift, industry, and Shaker traits of brotherly love and kindness. The Shakers failed to replace the young through other conversions. This loss—plus the industrial competition of an age with bigger machines than theirs—pushed the United Society past its prime.

Still, it had the gift to persist for another hundred years.

During the Civil War the Shakers again had to defend the pacifist principle that had been theirs since Mother Ann and her little band stood up to English and American mobs. They had a great spokesman in Elder Frederick William Evans, the best-known and most broad-minded of the later Shaker leaders. He was an English social reformer who emigrated to America in 1820 with his brother. Together they edited radical newspapers calling for land reform, women's rights, and the end of wage slavery. Interested in the utopian communities springing to life, Evans investigated them all. A strong personal mystical experience commended the Shakers, whom he joined in 1830.

Because his gift for leadership was recognized, Evans quickly leaped the ranks to become chief elder at New Lebanon. And from that Olympian post he urged the Shakers out of their traditional isolationist thinking and into the national movement for social reform. Many Believers thought him too worldly—and too conspicuous. He traveled abroad, carried on a wide correspondence with people like Tolstoy and

Henry George, wrote pamphlets on controversial public issues, and contributed articles to the national as well as the Shaker press.

President Lincoln found Evans an exceptionally able man when he went to Washington in 1863 to petition for draft exemption for the Shakers. He pointed out to the President that the Shakers had saved the United States Government more than half a million dollars. Many members who had fought in the Revolutionary War and the War of 1812 before becoming Shakers had never drawn their soldiers' pensions.

"Well," asked Lincoln, "what am I to do?"

"I can't advise the President," Elder Frederick answered.

"You ought to be made to fight," said Lincoln. "We need regiments of just such men as you!" Nevertheless, he granted the petition giving the brethren an indefinite furlough.

Neither warriors nor slaveholders, the western Shakers still suffered the ravages of the Civil War. Their homelands lay in the shifting battlefields of Kentucky and southern Ohio, and their trade was primarily with the South. The commune at South Union, Kentucky, served 50,000 meals to the hungry soldiers of both the Union and Confederate armies, who crowded to their kitchen doors and windows. And they lost $100,000 worth of buildings, livestock, and business, as well, through theft, maraaders, and money in bad debts.

This community had been founded on the site of the Kentucky Revival, which had brought so many souls into Shakerdom. Some of its first members were slaveholders who freed their slaves as soon as they joined the Shakers. Forty ex-slaves became Shakers, too. For many years they lived in a Negro commune with its own elder. From time to time some of them left for greater freedom, but many died in the faith. When the black commune grew too small, the members were taken in among the whites to live in integrated Shaker order. Negroes had been living in some white Northern communities for a long time. And a black family in Philadelphia was the first urban commune, with the sisters going out to work by day for the "world's people."

As much at home among the Shakers as blacks were former Jews, Catholics and Protestants, Adventists—as the Millerites were later called—and even nonbelievers and agnostics. The Shakers were always on the side of freethinkers and doubters, and opposed to rigid systems of religious belief.

Their leaders, or "leading characters," were early defenders of civil rights, constantly seeking tolerance, justice, and free speech for minority groups like themselves. They even defended the notorious Oneida Community in its religious communism of love. On his part, Oneida founder John Humphrey Noyes, in a book on American socialism, called the Shakers "the most influential social architects of modern times." He doubted whether his own or any of the other communities, religious and nonreligious, could ever have existed without their inspiration and example.

The Shakers were frequently called on by dignitaries like Edwin Stanton, Henry Clay—a western favorite—and Andrew Jackson, and commented on by literary visitors like Hawthorne, Melville, Emerson, Cooper, Howells, and Horace Greeley. Newspaper publisher Greeley was a happy patron of the American communal movement, especially the Fourieristic experiments in the phalanxes of the 1840's. In "association," he was confident, "the future may be assured."

Some admirers of Shaker socialism questioned the super-naturalism that remained an integral part of Shaker life. Elder Evans had to explain in a letter to Count Leo Tolstoy, that "spirit intercourse between parties in & out of mortal bodies" belonged primarily to the early church. The important thing for the author of *War and Peace* to realize was that a "poor illiterate, uneducated factory woman has confounded the wisdom of all *men*—reformers, legislators, and scholars, who have come to nothing as promoters of human happiness."

Evans urged him to found a Shaker order in Russia. But first he must come to New Lebanon to see how "we—the Shakers—under the American secular government carry out the . . . principles of the Christ spirit more perfectly than has ever been done by mortal men and women." He added, "Just as we carry out sexual purity, notwithstanding the sexes are brought face to face in everyday life, living without bars, in the same Household of Faith.

"See what God hath wrought!" he boasted. "Seventeen communities of people whose every right is secured to them, whose every rational want is supplied. . . . Our sisterhood are redeemed. The rights of women are theirs, the rights of property we enjoy. Capital and Labor are at peace. Hygiene is religion with us."

But the tall, stooped elder with his deep-set serious eyes had to watch the number of such fortunate people dwindle. Their energies, if not their advantages, decreased even as he spread their name. By now it was hard to maintain Shakerism at home, let alone sell it abroad, where he had tried a second time in England in 1880 at the age of seventy-nine.

Few were embracing the religious life that demanded so

Elder Frederick Evans was well known among the "world's people."

much of its members and kept them secluded in the country. There was more resignation than inspiration in some members' continued seeking of human perfection. With diminished numbers and reduced zeal, six Shaker villages closed between 1875 and 1900, and the surviving members moved to other communes. Some of the vast land holdings—each society had an average of 2,700 acres in 1875—were sold off or entrusted to hired hands. Many home industries were dropped, and the Shakers bought some of the assembly-line products of the world.

Elder Frederick shook his head when the looms stopped weaving Shaker cloth. "We buy more cheaply than we can make," he said, "but our homemade cloth is much better than what we can buy. And now we have to buy three pairs of trousers where before we made one. Thus our little looms would even now be profitable—to say nothing of the independence we secure in working them."

One new trend he favored was the broadening of Shaker life. The Believers began to read the world's newspapers and magazines, and books on science, history, and travel. They held reading meetings and had debating clubs. Purely pleasure-giving flowers and pictures and musical instruments were finally enjoyed. And why not? said Elder Evans. Saints deserved the good things of the world as much as sinners.

To hold the interest of the younger members, family problems were discussed in open meetings. But no one listened when young women wanted out of the kitchen, or yearned to let their hair grow free of the ever-present bonnets and indoor caps, which some in the West pushed back to their ears.

The only change allowed in the sisters' costume was the replacing of the separate shoulder kerchief with a yoke that still hid the bosom.

It was not until many years later that some of the sisters got their wish for less monotony. They had long outnumbered the brethren and were destined to outlast them. As the men grew fewer, the sisters took over more of the support of the families. They escaped from the communal kitchens and took to selling their confections in Shaker booths at country fairs. They became a familiar sight traveling in pairs to New England seaside, lake, and mountain resorts, where they peddled their small well-made wares and fancywork.

While Elder Frederick was busy at church headquarters with public relations, the quality and structure of local leadership elsewhere declined. Too many elders now wore two hats and, as part-time trustees, paid too little attention to spiritual matters. There were great financial losses, not only from uninsured fires and less productive farms, but from careless or foolish speculations and worldly investments, and even a lack of principle on the part of distracted leaders. Trying to hold things together, they neglected the faith and made things worse.

The old ingenuity and enterprise that once put the Shakers ahead of their time was declining. They became obsolete when machines separated man's hand from his work. Shakers could not understand a world that no longer saw work as an end in itself, a satisfying human activity. They could not keep up with such competition. Nor could they compromise. Shakers had "no middle way, no tolerance for halfway work," in Father Joseph's words. Labor was uniquely related to their worship of God, who was in every piece of wood, every garden. The motive was never profit, but the inspiration of the prophetess Mother Ann, the mother of their invention. Unfortunately, her voice was growing distant. There were no more Shakers who could hear it clearly or recall her unusual powers, like old Abijah Worster, the last survivor of the Harvard, Massachusetts, community. He carried to his grave this vivid memory:

"As I was tossing—tumbling—rolling—jumping—throwing myself against the wall—the chimney—the floor—the chairs, in fact everything that did not keep out of the way, I felt that my blood was boiling, and every bone in my body was being torn asunder, my flesh pinched with hot irons, and every hair on my head were stinging reptiles. I had laid me down to die, when Mother Ann came along, saying, 'Why, Abijah, there is some of the worst looking spirits on your shoulder I ever saw in my life.'

"I crawled along and laid me down at her feet and prayed her in mercy to help me; she raised me up and made a few resolute passes from my head to my feet, with her hands, and I was relieved at once,—and I have never doubted since."

Nor were there any left with the drive of Issachar Bates, who at fifty had walked back and forth between New England and Kentucky to found the western Shaker communes, and who later wrote: "My health is not very good, probably in consequence of having to travel seven miles every day to & from my work at the mill, sometimes in mud and water up to my knees, but my faith is everlasting and I mean to keep it."

Although they, too, kept the faith, they lost the fire, those latter-day Shakers following narrow paths through their communities and through life. When they went forth to worship, they were less nimble and spectacular than they had once been. They lost their audience, and by the end of the century they stopped dancing. The worship service moved out of the big empty meetinghouses and into upstairs rooms of the dwellings. Organ music helped the fewer and faded voices in thousands of simple hymns and vision songs they loved to sing.

In the early twentieth century the Shakers were condensed into fewer and fewer societies. Yet of all the nineteenth-century Yankee communes, only they had marched into the twentieth century with their convictions and communism intact. Much of the sturdy graceful furniture was sold, and some of the villages were occupied by institutions, schools, and churches. There, men and boys continued to live in the old communal buildings in the monastic order of which the Shakers approved.

"Do they marry?" Eldress Sarah Collins asked of the agent for a communal group that wanted to buy the South Family property at New Lebanon in the early 1940's. The applicant was a religious community driven out of Nazi Germany and welcomed in England until World War II. Now forced to leave Britain or be interned as enemy aliens, the Bruderhof, or Society of Brothers, wanted to settle in America.

Eldress Sarah thought it would be nice to have a Christian commune in the silent buildings—especially a pacifist one. The first great international peace conference had been sponsored by the Shakers at New Lebanon in 1905, with more than fifty nations represented. The new group, however, must not be the marrying kind.

It was.

"Nay, then it won't do," decided Eldress Sarah. "True communal living cannot be realized on the basis of the private family." She lived on till her nineties, as many Shakers did, and with fingers knotted from decades of chair-making, she built the last Shaker chair in 1947. A boy's school moved into New Lebanon.

The last Shaker brother died at Sabbathday Lake, Maine, in 1961. Fourteen sisters in their forties to nineties survive him there and at Canterbury, New Hampshire. These two communes, formerly considered "the least of Mother's children in the east," linger on in what one of them refuses to call the twilight of the Shaker faith. At Sabbathday Lake they see Shakerism as ongoing, "something that will last because something made it last, and because it is needed."

"The world needs our prayers," says tiny, white-haired Eldress Gertrude Soule at a private Sunday service in Maine. Her blue eyes peer through steel spectacles as she faces the aging sisters sitting on long benches in the spare upstairs chapel.

On the other side of the room from the sisters are a few male visitors and the resident museum director, a near-brother of this Shaker remnant. The only other onlookers are outside the tall shining windows—old maple trees, which the Shakers often planted, stretching across Route 26 out of Grey, off the Maine turnpike.

Sister R. Mildred Barker, a trustee in her seventies, and the family spokeswoman, plays the organ for the opening hymn. Then in her plain dark dress and thin white cap, she takes her official place on a bench behind the eldress, who also wears an indoor cap. The small congregation of sisters needs no further accompaniment. They sing with vigor and know by heart hundreds of the old songs, which they have recorded.

Most of the sisters no longer wear caps, and their hair is worn as they wish it. Their dresses are printed in small bright patterns in the same yoke-front style of seventy-five years ago, shortened a few inches above the ankle. Each sister makes a contribution to the service, a brief reading or a personal comment on self-improvement. Sister Mildred reflects aloud on some words of Mother Ann: "Heaven is a state of mind."

In that state of mind these serene sisters live. Nine older women on 1,900 acres sloping down to Sabbathday Lake, they sell the potato and corn crop, rent out the orchard of 2,000 trees, and freeze their own garden vegetables. During cold Maine winters they make small products to sell to visitors in the summer. They live by the bell in Shaker order, beginning with early morning prayer. They walk through one door of the common dining room, while the museum director goes through another; he and any men visiting sit down at a separate table.

Sister Mildred, who was brought to the Shakers at seven after her father died, receives the world's people in a room furnished with a row of old-fashioned rocking-chairs (none Shaker), one over-stuffed chair and a television set, which was a gift. For the Shakers of today, like those of yesterday, have many callers, correspondents, and friends. Some of her time is spent searching for Shaker furniture at country auctions and buying it back for the buildings that have become a

Sister Mildred Barker of the Sabbathday Lake community in Maine believes that Shakerism will last, because it is needed.

museum. Much of her time goes into the business management of a scholarly magazine called *The Shaker Quarterly*, published since 1961 at Sabbathday Lake.

At Canterbury, New Hampshire, the remaining sisters are older. There, until her recent death, lived Eldress Marguerite Frost, who more readily admitted that the Shakers have had their day—a good long one and a model to many. Of today's young people who seek a better way of life and come to visit the museum at Canterbury, where they have heard one once existed, this white-haired eldress used to say, "We have what they want." Many Millerites in the 1840's, who never got to heaven on either of the days they expected the world to end, found peace among the Shakers at Canterbury. "The Millerites," Eldress Marguerite noted, "made good Shakers." And she hoped that those turning away from the world today will find something with as lasting value as they did.

These fourteen sisters are the last of the Shakers, a special people born when they say the spirit of Christ made its second appearance in the humble person of Ann Lee. They are still trying to pass the word that the kingdom of God is now and that those in whom the true Christ spirit resides can always enter. They want the world's people—eager antique collectors of all things Shaker—to know about the religion and the communal way of life that inspired personal purity as well as manual perfection.

In big solid dwellings with double sets of doors and stairways, they still devote their lives to doing good and being good. And they continue to be as antiwar and socially aware as Shakers always have been. Not for many years have they taken in members or orphans, since the world now provides the welfare once offered by the Shakers. But they still love children, and a few little girls spend work vacations with them. Teen-age guides help out in the museum season, telling the Shaker adventure to tourists wandering through pristine restored rooms.

If the world is not yet ready for the good news that Mother Ann brought to America nearly 200 years ago, many thousands of people once were eager to receive it. Over the years, more than 70,000 men, women, and children dwelled among the Shakers and shared communal life on the model farms, although not all of them became members. And there is time, say these gentle Shaker sisters, for Shakerism or something akin to it to move and shake the world again.

To *Life* magazine, which pictured them as a dying sect and painted as grim a portrait of them as Charles Dickens once did, sprightly Sister Mildred wrote an indignant letter. "You missed the Brightness and Light which is Shakerism, the light, joy and vitality that is the product of Shakerism. Regardless of our numbers or our age, we have what the world is seeking and it will yet come into its own. What God has made alive will not stay buried."

The world surviving Mother Ann's children has inherited their many gifts. Out of the work of their hands has come a treasury of folk art, architecture, and music—an original American culture truly inspired by God and a way of life that was itself a religious service. Among other godsends were the gift to be simple and the gift of inspiration. The most important gift of all was the gift of community. Without it, the Shakers would have been just another American sect; with it, they became great.

In August of 1859 Sister Polly Collins of Hancock, Massachusetts, received a communication from the spirit world that inspired this drawing, "A Gift from Mother Ann to Eldress Eunice." Photographed by John McKee from the collection of the United Society of Shakers, Sabbathday Lake, Maine.

"Shaker Harmony," from a modern painting by Pennsylvania artist
Constantine Kermes, known for his portraits of "American saints."

AFTERWORD

Changes: The Shakers in the 1980s

More than two hundred years ago, on Sunday, September 26, 1784, the Marquis de Lafayette, on his way to help negotiate a peace treaty with the Indians of New York State, turned off at Niskayuna to see the Shaker worship.

The Shakers were so flattered by the attention of the twenty-two-year-old French hero of the American Revolution that they elevated his visit to a legend. They record a conversation between Lafayette and Mother Ann Lee in which she generously rejects his wish to become a Shaker until his work in this world is done.

On the same visit, Lafayette is said to have attached himself to Brother Abijah Worster of Harvard, Massachusetts, watching him closely as he danced "under operations of the power of God." This may be, for Abijah had come several weeks earlier to help bury Mother Ann. She had died on September 8. Mother Ann and Lafayette never met in this world.

Everyone loves legends and we are reluctant to unseat this one. But we learn the interesting truth from the diary of Francois de Barbé-Marbois, the French chargé d'affaires who accompanied Lafayette to the Shaker colony. Lafayette's curiosity about the Shakers sprang from an enthusiasm of his own. He was a mesmerist, a disciple and registered pupil of

Dr. Franz Anton Mesmer, who pioneered the development of hypnotism and was the sensation of Paris at that time.

Lafayette hoped that the Shakers would demonstrate the "secret invisible power in nature" called "animal magnetism," since they were known to heal disease by the laying-on of hands. He had tried with no success to "mesmerize" Brother Abijah.

Just as we cling to the legend of Lafayette's visit, so we cherish the old image of Shakerism itself. Yet Shakerism has never stood still. It has been growing and changing ever since Mother Ann and eight Believers in Christ's Second Appearing sailed into New York harbor on the ship *Mariah*, "two bright angels at the mast."

The Quaker Connection

Today even some basic assumptions in the story of the Shakers have changed. Scholars poking around the roots of the Shaker Tree of Life have discovered that neither the connection with the Quakers, with whom the Shakers are often confused, nor the relation to the Camisards and French Prophets, can be proved.

The Wardleys, lively James and Jane who welcomed twenty-two-year-old Ann Lee into their small society of religious dissenters in 1758, have always been called Quakers. But no confirmation of their Quaker faith has been found in the well-kept historical records of Friends in the Manchester area of England where they lived. Researchers have looked for all possible spellings of the name. "Wardley was an uncommon name in Manchester at that time, although there were Wardleys later," says Brother Theodore Johnson, director of the Shaker Library at Sabbathday Lake, Maine.

Another historian, Hillel Schwartz, has traced the fifty-year record of the 500 diverse French and English prophets and believers known as the French Prophets. He cannot confirm any Wardley attachment to the French Prophets or to the Quakers.

Then where did Shakerism come from, if not from Quakerism and the wonders and millenarial warnings of the Camisards and the French Prophets?

Manchester after the 1730s bubbled with religious excitement. The Quakers had quieted down, but the Methodists were stirring things up. George Whitefield, the powerful evangelist preacher whom Mother Ann once heard, and John Wesley, the founder of Methodism, turned the popular unrest in the industrializing city into a religious revival. Anxious seekers, hungry for more direct experience of God than the established Anglican Church provided, rushed from one source of "new light" to the next. They were influenced in their search by the mysticism of Jacob Boehme and the spiritualism of Emanuel Swedenborg.

Out of this growing eclecticism, Brother Ted Johnson suggests, "Shakerism coalesced into a distinct form from bits of native English dissent."

Baseball at the Burying Ground

A change of a different kind came to pass in 1983 in Colonie, New York, formerly known by the Indian name Niskayuna. Mother Ann lies in the thick of things in a Shaker cemetery around which the Albany airport grew. Now a baseball field borders the historic cemetery, although the Shakers and many others protested against its construction. Only a fence separates the Shaker graves from Heritage Park, with its minor league ball games, refreshment stands, and thousands of fans sitting on bleachers backed right up to the hallowed ground.

Mother Ann, in the third century of the religion she founded, is still honored by the Shakers, if not by the promoters of the Albany Colonie Yankees. Her few remaining "children" in two New England societies have seen some changes, too, and are traveling in different directions.

Since they celebrated the two-hundredth anniversary of her arrival in America, a renaissance of interest in the Shakers has put the keepers of the faith in the limelight. Even their differences are aired, although Shakers have been of two minds before. In the nineteenth century Elders Frederick Evans and Harvey Eads, representing liberal and conservative Shakerism, disagreed among other things about Shaker participation in the public arena. Others questioned the introduction of musical instruments into Shaker life and worship.

Now the issue of continuity is being faced matter-of-factly. The action at the Shaker village of Canterbury, New Hampshire, is in the museum; the action at Sabbathday Lake, Maine, is in the Shakers.

Canterbury: Old Order and New

At Canterbury three remarkably long-lived sisters have chosen to live in a museum-village run by a corporation with a twenty-member board and a full-time staff of twelve. The sisters are independent and lend the premises a healthy air of reality. Two of them are Eldresses in the Parent Ministry of the Millenial, or Shaker, Church.

Eldress Bertha Lindsay, a Shaker for more than eighty

years, speaks for the Canterbury community. She enjoys being consulted as village historian by Museum Director Richard Kathmann, Curator Bud Thompson, the herb specialist, the archivist and others. "I can't let go," she says. "Someone always wants to know something, things like, whose initials are these?"

In her late eighties and blind, she sits at a table with her tape recorder to report daily events, as Shakers have always done, and to communicate with distant friends. Many of her recollections of Canterbury are on tape in the village archives, descriptions of the household of a hundred members when she came as a child in 1905. Then there were twenty-five living in the branch family up the road, and seven mills, no longer in existence, were in operation.

Eldress Bertha's special talent is cooking and she is at work on a cookbook. Now she has help in the kitchen, besides the attention of Eldress Gertrude Soule, formerly of Sabbathday Lake, who lives with her and her fourteen-year-old dog, Penny, in the Trustees' Office. Both women wear the starched white indoor cap of Shaker tradition and put on bonnets when they leave home. They take good care of the caps because the French veiling from which they are made is no longer available.

The plants and knickknacks in their rooms belong to Eldress Gertrude, a sprightly nonagenarian. She uses the collection in the sitting room of stuffed toy animals, mostly gifts, when she tells stories to youngsters on the children's tours of the village.

Once these women worked hard at the many crafts for which industrious Shaker sisters were famous. Eldress Bertha says she made the last poplar box at Canterbury. But now

Eldresses Bertha Lindsay, above, and Gertrude Soule, right, at home in
the Trustees' Office at Shaker Village, Canterbury.

74

Photographs by Ken Williams, *Concord Monitor*

they have retired, except for taking turns greeting visitors who pass through the hall of the Eldresses' living quarters when they leave the reception center. "When all those visitors carry away the Shaker message," asks Eldress Bertha, "isn't that keeping Shakerism alive?"

The Canterbury sisters have not gathered for worship in many years. In the past they attended all the local and area churches. Now early on Sunday mornings the Eldresses watch a religious service on television.

The third sister lives apart with her fifteen-pound cat, Buster. Ethel Hudson came to Canterbury as "a kind of orphan" in 1907. She lived in the North and Second Families. Tiny, nearly ninety, she rarely dresses as a Shaker. It is not her "creation," she says quaintly, to greet many people, although she used to give tours of the village. When it is quiet, she sometimes emerges from her apartment in the fifty-six-room 1793 Dwelling House and walks down to visit Mildred Wells.

Mildred is a longtime resident of the village who came to this country from Hungary. Not a Covenant Shaker, she signed the Articles of Agreement to live with the Shakers and work without wages. Also in her eighties, she does the shopping for the three households and in the summer plants a big flower garden in her dooryard.

While the old order holds fast at Canterbury, the new order, the village corporation, continues restoration and improvement. Gradually, the twenty-two remaining buildings are receiving preservation treatments, and some have found new uses. The Creamery does a brisk business as a restaurant in the museum season. The Carriage House is a handsome gift shop and gallery, featuring exhibits such as "Blessed in Our

Basket," a display of Shaker containers from the Canterbury collection and other museums.

The 1792 Meeting House, used in the 1920s for entertainment, has been a display center since 1957 and continues in that role. The lane in front of it with its broad lawn shaded by maple trees is the scene of many Shaker anniversary celebrations, such as Mother Ann's Day. Other special events include concerts, Friends' Day and a family Christmas party.

Extending its cultural role, the village will host conferences of groups like the National Historic Communal Societies Association. Its newsletter is to become a magazine, and other publications are planned for 1986.

Probably the most important of these will be the final volumes summarizing an unusual historical and archeological survey of Canterbury Village. The first volume will map the once-extensive mill system explored at the sites of eight ponds formerly linked by ditching. According to archeologist David Starbuck, the survey's supervisor, these ponds provided enough power for a dozen mills during the community's peak in the nineteenth century. This industrial concept and its realization were on a grander scale than at any other Shaker village.

A second volume to emerge from the study will provide a user's list with captions of approximately 5,000 historic photographs and negatives that the researchers located. Eventually, two more books will describe architectural and population characteristics and changes.

One of the features of the landscape noted in a preliminary report is the stone water trough made by Brother Micajah Tucker in 1831 and placed at the foot of the hill at the approach to the village. Unused for many years and now filled with earth, the trough probably figured as the spring where the young runaway Shakers pause in Nathaniel Hawthorne's 1833 tale, "The Canterbury Pilgrims."

Hawthorne visited the Canterbury community and at one time half-thought of joining it. "On the whole, they lead a good and comfortable life," he wrote at the age of twenty-seven, "and if it were not for their ridiculous ceremonies, a man could not do a wiser thing than to join them."

The storybook village is set on 600 acres in rolling back country on a remote road in East Canterbury. Yet in 1985 more than 32,000 people made their way there.

Sabbathday Lake: "Come Life, Shaker Life"

The flow of visitors to Sabbathday Lake, Maine, hardly compares with the traffic to L.L. Bean, a half hour away. But those who are "mesmerized" by Shakerism seek out a second family of Believers at "Chosen Land."

These are Shakers who say they don't want to be remembered as furniture. A deeply religious community, they share a common purpose and try with useful celibate lives for the spiritual goodness of Mother Ann. They say "yea" and "nay" as she did.

On the Sabbath they welcome friends and neighbors to the 1794 Meeting House or to the chapel in the Brick Dwelling. Women sit with the sisters and men with the brethren. All are invited to speak when moved and to join in singing the old Shaker songs like "Let Me Have Mother's Gospel," "I Will Bow and Be Humble," and "Simple Gifts," a song for which Shakers are known the world over.

Work and worship fill their days, which begin with

morning prayers after breakfast and again before the noonday meal. They gather in late afternoon for further devotions and the study of Scripture. A second Shaker meeting in traditional form takes place on Wednesday evening.

Despite their religious vocation, these activist Shakers are not cloistered. Continuing a Maine tradition that began in the 1860s, they go to the fairs—local, state and regional—set up booths and sell their wares, mainly culinary herbs and herbal teas. They give cooking demonstrations, hold singing meetings, and lecture on all aspects of Shakerism.

At home they are farmers, raising sheep and growing herbs, vegetables and berries from the "grudging Maine soil." They benefit from rental of the orchard, and from a woodlot and three gravel pits on their 1900 acres.

They also operate a museum with a reception center, gift and bookshops, and tours of the trim old village of seventeen buildings. They additionally offer the community as a classroom for the serious study of Shakerism. The impressive contents of the Shaker Library are available to students, writers and researchers. Toward this end, an Institute of Shaker Studies has been established at the community. Courses conducted by Brother Ted Johnson receive college credit from the University of Southern Maine. Brother Ted, a big man with a big responsibility for the Maine Shaker Family, initiated and edited *The Shaker Quarterly*, published from 1961 through 1974. Publications by the community in 1986 will include his annotated collection of essays by Alonzo Hollister of Mount Lebanon, and notes accompanying an 1845 manuscript, "Sayings of Mother Ann and the First Elders," compiled by Roxalana L. Grosvenor of the Harvard, Massachusetts, society.

The Sabbathday Lake Shakers, singing "As the waves of the mighty ocean, Gospel love we will circulate," in traditional unaccompanied style, at Sunday meeting in the chapel of the 1883 Dwelling. From left to right, Sisters Marie Burgess, Elsie McCool, Frances Carr, Mildred Barker, and Minnie Greene, and Brothers Wayne Smith, Arnold Hadd and Ted Johnson.

The Sabbathday Lake Shakers have sponsored several conferences to enlarge understanding of the Shaker movement. The first, a three-day Bicentennial celebration of the Shakers' arrival in America in 1774, was a turning point in the history of the community. It attracted more than one hundred participants and rekindled the religious commitment of the Shaker Family. New friends gathered around them to

Photograph by Ann Chwatsky

share the peace and serenity of the ongoing Christian calling. A Friends of the Shakers organization sprang up and has met once a year ever since.

These friends and supporters, with historians and theologians who presented papers, participated in a second conference in 1980, observing the two-hundredth anniversary of the opening of the Shaker Gospel in America. In 1984 a third conference marked the bicentennial of the deaths of Mother Ann and her brother William Lee.

Events at Sabbathday Lake are enhanced by the hospitality of the sisters. Sister Frances Carr, the youngest Shaker sister, is the "kitchen deaconess" who has helped to make Shaker cooking popular with her workshops and her cookbook, *Shaker Your Plate*.

Other Family members include Sister Marie Burgess, whose running shoes suit her pace and who also puts her hands to work in the kitchen. Sister Minnie Greene leans on her cane, but is still indispensable to the "good room" where loaves of bread cool on upturned pans and meats roast in Shaker herbs. An older sister, Elsie McCool, now lives in a nearby nursing home.

Two young brothers in their twenties have cheered and energized community life, a reminder of the youthfulness and resourcefulness of Mother Ann's early converts. Brother Wayne Smith works on the farm, in the sheep barn, woodlot and garden. Brother Arnold Hadd is busy in the library, office, print shop, and often in the kitchen.

Shakers used to rotate jobs, but today Family members work wherever help is needed, as well as where they work best. They pack herbs into tins, wrap gift items to fill mail orders, pick berries, bake and prepare for the popular annual Christmas Fair, or mount an exhibition.

It helps to have a full-time staff of two, an archivist and a curator of collections. And good friends like Ruth Nutter, a former Shaker sister who has kept the Shaker store on the road for many years.

Sister Frances Carr gathers herbs in a large oval carrier.

The animal family at Sabbathday Lake has a supporting role, too. Besides a flock of sheep and a ram, there are two large dogs, three geese, a rooster, and, upstairs in Sister Mildred's neat room, a canary named Joy.

Sister Mildred Barker, nearing ninety, continues to run up and down stairs in the 1883 Dwelling, and to hurry from the Dwelling to the Office to accomplish her multiple tasks as Trustee. More than eighty years a Shaker, she has not wavered from her faith. "I gave a promise as a little girl to 'make a Shaker,' " she says, "and I have never been sorry." She has seen many changes since Shakerism marched into modern times. "Those in power don't understand," she insists. "Shakerism will never die, even if people fail it."

The Gift of Song

Sister Mildred taught the Sabbathday Lake Shakers many of the old songs she learned as a child among Believers at Alfred, Maine. She won a National Heritage Fellowship in 1984 for her devotion to keeping alive this rich inheritance of Shaker song, much of it based on early American and English folk tunes.

Shaker songs outnumber those of any other denomination, according to Dr. Daniel Patterson, author of *The Shaker Spiritual*. He has located and studied more than 10,000 songs in 800 manuscripts still in existence.

In *Gift Drawing and Gift Song*, published by the Maine Shakers in 1983, Dr. Patterson notes that the same revival period in the 1840s that inspired an abundance of songs produced far fewer gift drawings. Only 192 Shaker religious art works are known, partly because the Shakers, like most Americans, lacked as strong a tradition in the decorative arts as in music. The drawings, despite their dramatic messages from the spirit world, had little communal use and a short life. Once viewed, they were laid aside and forgotten. By contrast, songs could be learned quickly and became common property, "living on in every memory and voice and every community." Many are alive today in Shaker worship.

World of "Shaker"

The few Shaker artists, mostly women, who set down their heavenly visions would be astonished to see "cutout ornaments" from them advertised in the pages of a Shaker-news magazine. *The Shaker Messenger* reflects a world of "Shaker." Interest in the Believers and enthusiasm for both Shaker and Shaker-like arts and crafts create a growing public for Shaker-related products, books, study groups, conferences, seminars, exhibitions and entertainment. Further enlarging this public, a documentary film about the Shakers by Ken and Amy Burns was viewed on national public television in 1985 by an estimated 6.9 million people.

Since the cost of Shaker antiques has risen to awesome heights, reproductions offer an alternative. And so well made are some of them that a two-year-old oblong carrier was sold for $3800 at a 1985 antiques auction before its provenance was discovered. The box originated at Hancock Shaker Village in Pittsfield, Massachusetts, where skilled artisans work in restored community settings.

Shaker Showplaces

Hancock is one of the showplaces that have stimulated national interest in the Shakers. Tucked into the cultural heart of the Berkshires, it beckons thousands of vacationers into a quiet, tidy realm of barns (including the famous Round Barn), shops, pastures and herb gardens surrounding a tall brick communal dwelling. The museum offers a calendar full of educational and entertaining programs from antique shows to World's People's Dinners. Many of the original gift drawings can be seen there.

Two other Shaker villages have been recreated, both in Kentucky. Transformed from acres of run-down property, Shakertown at Pleasant Hill has developed into the Williamsburg of the Shaker museums and the largest. In 1985 more than 128,000 people toured the community, open year 'round with lodging and meals in Shaker buildings. A special attraction is a trip down the Kentucky River from Shaker Landing on the paddlewheeler Dixie Belle.

A more intimate museum-village, Shakertown at South Union, Kentucky, was launched in 1971 when a private collection was moved into the 1824 Centre House. The museum now includes a former Shaker-owned tavern on the railroad and a Shaker post office down the road. Every year visitors enjoy a play called "Shakertown Revisited" during a summer festival.

The restored villages, and the ongoing ones at Canterbury and Sabbathday Lake, share a typical elegance and simplicity and order. But there are more than regional differences among them.

Once it was assumed that the Shaker communes were alike, based on the pattern of industry established at Mount Lebanon, the mother-church in New York. Mount Lebanon encompassed eight families and an incredible range of productivity within them. But while Shaker business methods may have been copied from east to west, as exterior Shaker architecture was, communal expression varied from one society to another. The Believers, after all, were individuals, not paper dolls in bonnets and broad-brimmed hats dancing across the country.

Men and women came to Shaker life over many paths. They brought to it strengths and weaknesses from their former lives. Despite their union, an important Shaker goal, they were not nameless. Curator-at-large June Sprigg argues a new viewpoint, that much of the furniture they produced was signed and not anonymous. (Nor was all of it, comments another curator, "religion in wood.")

As an example of the diversity of communities, Canterbury, Richard Kathmann says, was "sounder economically" at the turn of the century than most of the other societies. It was a "counterpoint" to Mount Lebanon. The Believers at Sabbathday Lake, on the other hand, four times considered moving to a more hospitable terrain. Yet they mustered strong powers of survival.

Less durable than these New England communities, Mount Lebanon as the home of Believers closed down in 1947 and the few surviving members moved over the mountain to Hancock in Massachusetts. The role of the central ministry had already been transferred to Hancock. Later Canterbury assumed "the lead."

A boys' school settled into Mount Lebanon and its successor, the Darrow School, remains in residence. An active religious group called the Abode of the Message, believers in Sufism, occupy the South Family dwellings, and restoration of other structures is under way to create another Shaker showplace, Mount Lebanon Shaker Village.

Thus, the old Shaker communities serve a variety of uses. They have all become, wholly or in part, museums, schools, religious institutions, correctional facilities, retirement homes, state or private property.

The museum-villages in the east and west and other spaces where Shakers used to work and worship are oases on the American scene. Shaker homes always were a phenomenon. People flocked to see the self-sufficient, socially-advanced hamlets that had no poverty, no crime, no jails, where women as well as men governed and enjoyed equal opportunities.

The Shakers of the past, as now, presented a social alternative with a big price. But in more religious times, celibacy, rewarded by salvation and in the good company of others with a like calling, was not unappealing.

The communal scheme was essential to Shaker independence, creativity and invention. If Mother Ann had lived beyond the age of 48, would the Shakers, without the meticulous communal organization of her first American successor, Father Joseph Meacham, be among us today?

If you should be so persecuted, as to have your houses torn down over your heads, and you cast out into the fields, you must not neglect meeting together to serve God. And if you never see my face any more, nor the faces of any that are with me from England, you have those whom God has raised up, among yourselves, who are able to lead you in the way of God, if you will obey them.

—Mother Ann Lee, *Testimonies of the Life, Character, Revelation and Doctrines of Our ever Blessed Mother Ann Lee, and the Elders with Her; through whom the Word of Eternal Life was Opened in this Day of Christ's Second Appearing....1816.*

~

A visitor sits on a long bench on the sisters' side of the white-painted, blue-bordered Meeting House at Sabbathday Lake. Facing the brethren and male guests, she avoids their eyes, as sisters must always have been supposed to do. She studies the high ceiling, the clock on a shelf, the long-necked black stove on its little cat feet, the worn wood floor where Believers used to dance and march. Tall grass waves outside the windows, and 2400 apple trees are in bloom on the hill behind the Meeting House.

She returns her gaze to the neat coil of gray hair at the back of Sister Mildred's bowed head, and to the small calico cheerfulness of Sister Minnie's lavender dress with its ample layered yoke. Sister Marie wears pink and Sister Frances blue that matches her eyes. Brother Wayne wears chinos and a blue smock from an old Shaker brethren's pattern. He sits with his arms folded across his chest.

Brother Arnold slips in through the men's doorway and takes his seat next to Brother Ted. He has locked the doors of the Brick Dwelling across the road.

Shaker meeting begins with the singing of Hymn XII, "The Shakers," from Part IV of the first hymn book, *Millenial Praises*, published without music in 1813. The preface of that book says,

> As the work of regeneration is an increasing work, and as there can be no end of the increase in God's government and Kingdom; so all that his people have to do is, to keep in the increasing work of God, and unite with whatever changes that increase may lead to, which, to the truly faithful, will be a continual travel from grace to grace, and from glory to glory.

THE SHAKERS

1. *When the Lord in ancient days,*
   Set Mount Sinai in a blaze,
   O, the trumpet's awful sound!
   How it shook the solid ground!

CHORUS: *Shaking here, and shaking there,*
   People shaking everywhere,
   Since I have my sins confess'd,
   I can shake among the rest.

2. *When the burning flames appear'd,*
   Guilty rebels shook and fear'd;
   Now we see a hotter blaze,
   Kindled in these latter days.

CHORUS: *Shaking here, and shaking there . . .*

3. *Now the flame begins to run,*
   Now the shaking is begun,
   He that gave creation birth,
   Shakes the heavens and the earth.

CHORUS: *Shaking here, and shaking there . . .*

4. *Tho' the wicked stand and mock,*
   They shall not escape the shock;
   All the world will have to say,
   Shaking is no foolish play.

CHORUS: *Shaking here, and shaking there . . .*

5. *We'll be shaken to and fro,*
   Till we let old Adam go;
   When our souls are born again,
   We unshaken shall remain.

CHORUS: *Shaking here, and shaking there . . .*

6. *Some will boldly try to stand,*
   But the Lord will shake the land;
   Sinners who shall dare rebel,
   Will be shaken into hell.

WHERE TO FIND SHAKER COLLECTIONS IN MUSEUMS AND LIBRARIES*

MUSEUMS and PUBLIC COLLECTIONS

DELAWARE
   The Henry Francis du Pont Winterthur Museum, Winterthur 19735

KENTUCKY
   Kentucky Museum, Bowling Green 42101
   Shakertown at Pleasant Hill, Harrodsburg 40330
   Shakertown at South Union 42283

MAINE
   Shaker Museum, United Society of Shakers, Sabbathday Lake, Poland Spring 04274

MASSACHUSETTS
   Fruitlands Museums, Harvard 01451
   Hancock Shaker Village, Pittsfield 01201
   Museum of Fine Arts, Boston 02115

NEW HAMPSHIRE
   Shaker Museum, Shaker Inn, Lower Shaker Village, Enfield 03748
   Shaker Museum, Shaker Village Inc., Canterbury 03224

---

*This list updates the basic *Shaker Museum Guide to Shaker Collections & Libraries*, published by the Shaker Museum at Old Chatham, New York.

NEW YORK

Metropolitan Museum of Art, American Wing, New York City 10028
Mount Lebanon Shaker Village, New Lebanon 12125
Shaker Heritage Society, Albany 12211
Shaker Museum, Old Chatham 12136

OHIO

Dunham Tavern Museum, Cleveland 44106
Golden Lamb Hotel, Lebanon 45036
Kettering-Moraine Museum, Kettering 45439
Ohio Historical Society, Columbus 43211
Shaker Historical Society Museum, Shaker Heights 44120
Warren County Historical Society Museum, Lebanon 45036
Western Reserve Historical Society, History Museum, Cleveland 44106

PENNSYLVANIA

Philadelphia Museum of Art 19130

VERMONT

Shelburne Museum, Shelburne 05482

WISCONSIN

Milwaukee Art Museum, Villa Terrace 53202

ENGLAND

The American Museum, Claverton Manor, Bath BA2 7BD

SHAKER LIBRARY COLLECTIONS

CONNECTICUT

Connecticut State Library, Hartford 06115

DELAWARE

   The Henry Francis du Pont Winterthur Museum Library,
   Winterthur 19735

DISTRICT OF COLUMBIA

   Library of Congress 20540

INDIANA

   Indiana Historical Society Library, Indianapolis 46202

KENTUCKY

   Filson Club, Louisville 40203
   Kentucky Library, Bowling Green 42101
   Shakertown at South Union 42283
   University of Kentucky, Margaret I. King Library, Lexington
   40506
   Western Kentucky University, Kentucky Library, Bowling Green
   42101

MAINE

   Shaker Library, United Society of Shakers, Sabbathday Lake 04274

MASSACHUSETTS

   American Antiquarian Society, Worcester 01609
   Berkshire Athenaeum, Pittsfield 02101
   Fruitlands Museums Library, Harvard 01451
   Hancock Shaker Village, Pittsfield 01201
   Massachusetts Historical Society, Boston 02215
   Williams College, Sawyer Library, Williamstown 01267

MICHIGAN

   University of Michigan, William L. Clements Library, Ann Arbor
   48109

NEW HAMPSHIRE
New Hampshire Historical Society Library, Concord 03301
Dartmouth College, Baker Library, Hanover 03755

NEW YORK
Buffalo and Erie County Public Library, Buffalo 14203
Hofstra University Library, Hempstead, Long Island 11550
New York Public Library, New York City 10018
New York State Library, Albany 12230
Shaker Museum, Emma B. King Library, Old Chatham 12136
Syracuse University, George Arents Research Library,
Syracuse 13210

NORTH CAROLINA
Duke University, William R. Perkins Library, Durham 27706

OHIO
Dayton and Montgomery County Public Library, Dayton 45402
Massilon Public Library, Massilon 44646
Miami University, Walter Havighurst Special Collections Library,
Oxford 45056
Ohio Historical Society Library, Columbus 43211
Shaker Heights Public Library, Shaker Heights 44120
Shaker Historical Society, Shaker Heights 44120
Warren County Historical Society Library, Lebanon 45036
Western Reserve Historical Society, History Library,
Cleveland 44106

WISCONSIN
State Historical Society of Wisconsin, Madison 53706

OTHER BOOKS OF INTEREST

BY THE SHAKERS

Bates, Paulina. *The Divine Book of Holy and Eternal Wisdom, Revealing the Word of God; Out of Whose Mouth Goeth a Sharp Sword*. In two vols. Canterbury, N.H.: 1849.

Bishop, Rufus. *Testimonies of the Life, Character, Revelations and Doctrines of Our ever Blessed Mother Ann Lee, and the Elders with Her* . . . Hancock: Printed by J. Tallcott & J. Deming, 1816.

Green, Calvin, and Seth Y. Wells. *A Summary View of the Millenial Church, or United Society of Believers, (Commonly Called Shakers)*. Albany: Printed by Packard & Van Benthuysen, 1823. Revised edition, Albany, 1848.

Johnson, Brother Theodore E. *In the Eye of Eternity: Shaker Life and the Work of Shaker Hands*. Gorham, Maine: The United Society of Shakers and the University of Southern Maine, 1983.

McNemar, Richard. *The Kentucky Revival: or, a short history of the late extraordinary outpouring of the spirit of God in the western states of America* . . . *with a brief account of the entrance and progress of what the world calls Shakerism among the subjects of the late revival in Ohio and Kentucky* . . . . Cincinnati: 1807. Reprint, Albany, 1808. Reprint, New York: AMS Press, 1974.

The Shaker Quarterly, Sabbathday Lake, Poland Spring, Maine: Published by the United Society. Portland, Maine: Anthoensen Press, 1961–1974.

Wells, Seth Youngs, and Calvin Green. *Testimonies Concerning the Character and Ministry of Mother Ann Lee and the First Witnesses of the Gospel of Christ's Second Appearing....* Albany, N.Y.: Printed by Packard & Van Benthuysen, 1827.

Wells, Seth Youngs, comp. *Millenial Praises, Containing a Collection of Gospel Hymns, in Four Parts; Adapted to the Day of Christ's Second Appearing. Composed for the use of his people.* Hancock: Printed by Josiah Tallcott, Junior, 1813.

Wells, Rufus, and Seth Y. Wells, eds. *Testimonies of the Life, Character, Revelations and Doctrines of Mother Ann Lee, and the Elders with Her....* Second edition, revised by Giles B. Avery. Albany, N.Y.: Weed, Parsons & Co., Printers, 1888.

White, Anna, and Leila S. Taylor. *Shakerism: Its Meaning and Message.* Columbus, Ohio: 1904.

Youngs, Benjamin Seth. *The Testimony of Christ's Second Appearing; Containing a General Statement of All Things Pertaining to the Faith and Practice of the Church of God in This Latter-day....* Lebanon, Ohio: 1808. Revised and expanded editions: Albany, 1810; Union Village, Ohio, 1823; Albany, 1856.

ABOUT THE SHAKERS

Andrews, Edward Deming. *The Community Industries of the Shakers.* Reprint, Charlestown, Mass.: Emporium Publications, 1972.

_____ . *The Gift to be Simple: Songs, Dances and Rituals of the American Shakers.* New York: Dover, 1967.

Butler, Linda, and June Sprigg. *Inner Light: The Shaker Legacy.* New York: Alfred A. Knopf, 1985.

Chase, Eugene Parker, trans. and ed. *Our Revolutionary Forefathers: The Letters of Francois, Marquis de Barbé-Marbois During his Residence in the United States as Secretary of the French Legation, 1779–1785.* New York: Duffield & Co., 1929.

Desroche, Henri. *The American Shakers.* Trans. and ed. John K. Savacool. Amherst, Mass.: University of Massachusetts Press, 1971.

Clark, Thomas D., and F. Gerald Ham. *Pleasant Hill and Its Shakers.* Second edition, Pleasant Hill Press, 1983.

Dickens, Charles. *American Notes for General Circulation.* Chap. 15. London: Chapman and Hall, 1842. Reprint, New York: St. Martin's Press, 1985.

Filley, Dorothy M. *Recapturing Wisdom's Valley: The Watervliet Shaker Heritage.* New York: Publishing Center for Cultural Resources, 1975.

Gottschalk, Louis. *Lafayette Between the American and the French Revolution.* Chicago: University of Chicago Press, 1950.

Harrison, J.F.C. *The Second Coming: Popular Millenarianism 1780–1850.* New Brunswick, N.J.: Rutgers University Press, 1979.

Hinds, William Alfred. *American Communities.* Oneida, N.Y.: 1878. Reprinted 1902, 1908. New York: Corinth Books, 1961.

Marini, Stephen A. *Radical Sects of Revolutionary New England.* Cambridge, Mass.: Harvard University Press, 1982.

Melcher, Marguerite Fellows. *The Shaker Adventure*. Princeton: Princeton University Press, 1941. Reprint, Old Chatham, New York: Shaker Museum, 1980.

Miller, Amy Bess. *Hancock Shaker Village: The City of Peace*. Dalton, Mass.: Studley Press, 1984.

Morse, Flo. *The Shakers and the World's People*. New York: Dodd, Mead and Company, 1980.

Muller, Charles R., and Timothy D. Reiman. *The Shaker Chair*. Published by the Canal Press, Canal Winchester, Ohio. Dalton, Mass.: Studley Press, 1984.

Neal, Julia. *The Kentucky Shakers*. Lexington, Ky.: University Press of Kentucky, 1977.

Nordhoff, Charles. *The Communistic Societies of the United States*. New York: Harper & Brothers, 1875. Reprints, Dover, 1966; Corner House, Wellfleet, Mass., 1978.

Noyes, John Humphrey. *History of American Socialisms*. Philadelphia: J.B. Lippincott & Co., 1870. Reprint, New York, Hillary House, 1961.

Patterson, Daniel W. *Gift Drawing and Gift Song*. Published by the United Society of Shakers, Sabbathday Lake, Maine. Portland, Maine: Anthoensen Press, 1983.

———. *Six Gift Drawings*. (A portfolio of plates from *Gift Drawing and Gift Song*.) Sabbathday Lake, Maine: The United Society of Shakers, 1985.

———. *The Shaker Spiritual*. Princeton, N.J.: Princeton University Press, 1979.

Pearson, Elmer R., and Julia Neal. *The Shaker Image*. Boston: New York Graphic Society and Shaker Community, Inc., 1974.

Piercy, Caroline B. *The Valley of God's Pleasure: A Saga of the North Union Shaker Community*. New York: Stratford House, 1951.

Richmond, Mary L., compiler and annotator. *Shaker Literature: A Bibliography*, in two volumes. Hanover, N.H.: Published by Shaker Community, Inc. and University Press of New England, 1977.

Sasson, Diane. *The Shaker Spiritual Narrative*. Knoxville, Tenn.: University of Tennessee Press, 1983.

Sears, Clara Endicott. *Gleanings From Old Shaker Journals*. Boston: Houghton Mifflin Company, 1916. Reprint, Hyperion, Westport, Conn., 1975.

Schwartz, Hillel. *The French Prophets: The History of a Millenarian Group in Eighteenth-Century England*. Berkeley, Los Angeles, London: University of California Press, 1980.

Van Kolken, Diana. *Introducing the Shakers—An Explanation & Directory*. Bowling Green, Ohio: Gabriel's Horn Publishing Co., 1985.

Whitworth, John McKelvie. *God's Blueprints: A Sociological Study of Three Utopian Sects*. London and Boston: Routledge & Kegan Paul, 1975.

FOR FURTHER READING

FICTION ABOUT THE SHAKERS

Deland, Margaret. *The Way to Peace*. New York: Harper & Bros., 1910.

Giles, Janice Holt. *The Believers*. Boston: Houghton Mifflin Company, 1957. Reprint, New York: Avon Books, 1976.

Hawthorne, Nathaniel. "The Canterbury Pilgrims," in *The Token and Atlantic Souvenir*. Boston: American Stationers' Company, 1833. Collected in *The Snow Image and Other Twice-told Tales*. Boston: Ticknor, Reed and Fields, 1852.

———. *"The Shaker Bridal,"* in *Twice-told Tales*. Boston: American Stationers' Co., 1837. Also in *The Token and Atlantic Souvenir*, Boston: 1838.

———. Both stories appear in *The Complete Novels & Selected Tales of Nathaniel Hawthorne*. Ed., Norman Holmes Pearson. New York: The Modern Library, 1937

Holden, Marietta. *The Story of Martha, or Love's Ordeal*. Boston: American Printing Co., 1909. (Published as *Uncovered Ears and Opened Vision*, by "The Princess," 1904)

Howells, William Dean. *The Undiscovered Country*. Boston: Houghton Mifflin Company, 1880.

———. *The Day of Their Wedding*. New York: Harper & Brothers, 1895.

———. *A Parting and a Meeting*. New York: Harper & Brothers, 1896.

_____ . *The Vacation of the Kelwyns: An Idyll of the Middle Seventies.* New York: Harper & Brothers, 1920.

Jonas, Gerald. "The Shaker Revival," (science fiction) *Galaxy* Magazine, February, 1970.

Leslie, Ann George. *Dancing Saints.* Garden City, N.Y.: Doubleday, Doran and Co., 1943.

Sears, Clara Endicott. *The Romance of Fiddler's Green.* Boston and New York: Houghton Mifflin Company, 1922.

Sedgwick, Catharine Maria. *Redwood: A Tale.* New York: E. Bless and E. White, 1824. Reprint, New York: Garrett Press, Inc., 1969.

Wiggin, Kate Douglas. *Susanna and Sue.* Boston: Houghton Mifflin Company, 1909.

Yolen, Jane. *The Gift of Sarah Barker.* (Juvenile) New York: Viking Press, 1981.

Zaroulis, Nancy. *Call the Darkness Light.* New York: Doubleday and Company, 1979. Reprint, Signet, New American Library, 1980.

INDEX

Page numbers in italics indicate illustrations.

Adventists, 55. *See also* Millerites
Agriculture. *See* Farms and farming
Albany, New York, 7, 10, 11
    Albany airport, 71
Alcott, Bronson, 30
Alcott, Louisa May, 30
Alfred, Maine, Shaker community at, 18, 84
American Notes for General Circulation
    (Dickens), 33, 34
Anglican Church, 4, 71
"Animal Magnetism," 70. *See also*
    Mesmerism
Antiques, 65, 85, 86
Apostates, 47
Architecture, 19, 21, 40, 52, 61, 76, 77, 78,
    84, 86, 87
    meetinghouses, 16–17, 19, 31, 61, 77, 78,
    89
Art, religious. *See* Gift drawings
Arts and crafts. *See* Furniture and artifacts,
    arts and crafts
Articles of Agreement, 76

Barbé-Marbois, Francois, Marquis de, 69
Barker, Sister R. Mildred, 62–64, 65, 66,
    80, 84, 89
Baptists, 10, 11
Bates, Issachar, 23, 26–27, 60
Believers in Christ's Second Appearing,
    United Society of, 5, 17, 27, 70
Biblical references, *xi*
Bicentennial, Shakers' arrival in America,
    72, 80
Black Shakers, 26, 54–55
Blithedale Romance, The, 30

Boehme, Jacob, 71
Borden, Gail, 48
Brook Farm, 30
Brooms, *18–19*, 35, 36, 48, 52
    spiritual, 35, 42
Burns, Ken and Amy, 85
Burgess, Sister Marie, *80*, 82, 89
Business, 36, 87. *See also* Work
Busro (West Union), Indiana, Shaker
    community at. 27–28

Camisards, 4, 70, 71
Canterbury, New Hampshire, Shaker
    community at, *xiii*, 18, 20, *51*, 62, 65,
    72–73, *74–75*, 76–78, 86, 87
    archeological and historical survey, 77–78
    Hawthorne on, 78
    mill system, 77
    village corporation, 76
"Canterbury Pilgrims, The," 78
Carr, Sister Frances, *80*, 82, *83*, 89
Celibacy, 2, 10, 15, 20, 23, 28, 38, 45, 47,
    56, 65, 88. *See also* Separation of sexes
Chairs. *See* Furniture and artifacts
Changes in Shakers and Shakerism, 59, 69,
    70, 71, 72, 90
Characteristics of Shakers, 29, 36, 53, 59
Charity, 49, 54
Children, 20, 34, 44, 48–49, *49*, 50, *51*,
    52–53, 66
    orphans, 48–49, 66
    spiritual, 27, 35, 38
Christ spirit, 3, 4, 10, 12, 17, 56, 65
Civil War, 47, 53, 54
Clay, Henry, 55
Cohoon, Sister Hannah, 41
Collins, Eldress Sarah, 61–62
Colonie, New York, 71

Communal organization and society order, 18, 20, 21, 23, 41, 63, 88

Communism, religious, *xi*, 2, 14, 15, 16, 20, 23, 25, 29, 30, 55, 61–62, 65–66

Communities, Shaker, *xiii*, 17, 23, 26–28, 37, 39, 47–48, 56, 58, 60, 86–88. *See also specific communities*

Communitarianism, 1–2, 30–31, 55, 62, 66

Confession of sin, 12, 23, 25, 26–27, 35

Converts, 10–13, 15–18, 26, 38, 47, 49, 53

Cooking, Shaker, 10, *24*, 48, 52, 54, 59, 73, 79, 82, 86

Cooper, James Fenimore, 55

Covenant, Shaker, 23, 47, 53, 76

Cunningham, family named, 6–7

Daily life, Shaker, 22, 48, 52, 56, 58–59, 63, 65–66

Dancing, worship in, 2, 3, 6, 10, 22, 31, 35, *36*, 40, 42, 44, *45*, 45, 46, 61, 89

Darrow School, 88

Decline, of Shakers, 56, 58, 61

Dickens, Charles, 33–34, 36, 66

Discipline, 16, 20, 89

Dress, 6–7, *12–13*, *18–19*, 20, 21, 22, 24, 28, *29*, 34, *36*, 39, 45, *45*, 46, 49, 57, 58–59, 62–63, 64, 73, *74–75*, *80–81*, 87, 89

Eads, Elder Harvey, 72

Education, 50, 52

Emerson, Ralph Waldo, 55

Enfield, Connecticut, Shaker community at, 17, 18

Enfield, New Hampshire, Shaker community at, 18

Equality
  racial, 2, 30
  sexual, 2, 17, 20, 30, 47
  See also Women's rights, Black Shakers

Evans, Elder Frederick William, 53–54, 56, *57*, 58, 59, 72

Families, Shaker 20, 28–29, 48, 58, 76, 78, 80, 82, 87

Farms and farming, 24, 28–29, 30, 59, 66, 79, 82

Feminism. *See* Equality, sexual; Women, Women's rights

Friends. *See* Quakers

Friends of the Shakers, 81

French Prophets, 70, 71. *See also* Camisards

Fruitlands, 30

Fourier, Charles, 30
  Fourieristic phalanxes, 55

Fox sisters, 44. *See also* Spiritualism

Frost, Eldress Marguerite, 65

Furniture and artifacts, arts and crafts, 34, 36, 39, 40, 52, 61, 62, 64, 73, 77, 78, 87, 89. *See also* Brooms

George, Henry, 54

"Gifts," Shaker, 5, 27, 38, 40, 43, 50, 66

Gift drawings, 40–41, *42* ("Tree of Life"), 67 ("A Gift from Mother Ann to Eldress Eunice"), 85, 86

God, 3, 4, 5, 6, 7, 9, 10, 16, 22, 25, 35, 37, *45*, 53, 66, 69, 71, 88
  Kingdom of, 15, 19, 29, 65, 90
  as Mother and Father, 2
  way of, 11, 15, 89

Goodrich, Elizur, 17

Gorham, Maine, Shaker community at, 18

Gospel, Shaker, 7, 78
  "travel" in the, 23
  bicentennial of opening of, 81
  gospel order, 21

Government and leadership, 17, 20, 47, 55, 59, 89

Great awakening, 9

Greeley, Horace, 55

Greene, Sister Minnie, *80*, 82, 89

Grosvenor, Roxalana L., 79

Hadd, Brother Arnold, *80–81*, 82, 89

Hancock, Massachusetts, Shaker community at, 18, 87
  "City of Peace," 41
  Hancock Shaker Village (museum village), 85–86

Harvard, Massachusetts, 12
  Shaker community at, 18, 69, 79
Hawthorne, Nathaniel, 30, 55, 78
Healing practices, 10, 70
Herbs, 22, 36, 52, 79, 82, 83, 86
Heritage Park, 71
Hocknell, Father John 5, 7, 15
Hollister, Elder Alonzo, 79
Holy, Sacred and Divine Rock and Roll, A, 43
Housecleaning, Shaker, 10, 35, 46–47, 52
Howells, William Dean, 55
Hudson, Sister Ethel, *ix*, 76
Hygiene, 47, 56
Hypnotism, 70. *See also* Mesmerism

Indiana, 27, 28, 30
Indians, 28, 38, 69
Industry, 53, 58, 87. *See also* Work
Inspiration, 32, 33, 40. *See also* Spiritualism
Institute of Shaker Studies, 79
Inventions, 48, 59, 60, 88

Jackson, Andrew, 55
Jesus, 4, 37
Johnson, Brother Moses, 19
Johnson, Brother Theodore E., 70, 71, 79, 80–81, 89

Kathmann, Richard, 73, 87
Kentucky, 23, 27, 54, 60, 86
Kentucky Revival, 23, 25, 54

Lafayette, Marquis de, 69, 70
Lee (Lees), Mother Ann, 3–4, 8, 16, 17, 21, 22, 27, 38, 40, 41, 43, 53, 56, 63, 65, 66, 67, 70, 82
  death of, 15
  at first American settlement at Niskayuna, 7, 9
  grave, 18, 71
  and Lafayette, 69
  marriage, and death of children, 5, 7
  missionary trip, 11–14

Lee, Mother Ann *(cont'd)*
  passage to America, 5–6
  persecution in England, 4–5
  prophecies, 9, 15, 23
  sayings, 7, 14–15, 19, 31, 50, 52, 79, 88–89
  in Shaker theology, 3–4, 10, 12, 35, 37, 60, 72
Lee (Lees), Nancy, 5
Lee (Lees), Father William, 5, 14, 15, 82
Life magazine, 66
Lincoln, Abraham, 54
Lindsay, Eldress Bertha, 72, 73, 74, 76

Manchester, England, 3, 4, 70, 71
Mariah, the ship, 3, 5–6, 70
McCool, Sister Elsie, 80, 82
McNemar, Elder Richard, 25, 43
Meacham, John, 25
Meacham, Father Joseph, 10, 15, 17, 22, 23, 59, 88
Melville, Herman, 55
Membership, 2, 29, 47, 66
Mesmer, Dr. Franz Anton, 70
Mesmerism, 69, 70, 78
Methodists, 71
Millennial, or Shaker, Church, 5, 41, 42, 72
Millennial Praises, 3, 89–91
Millennialism, heaven on earth, 1, 9, 29, 37, 65
Miller, the Rev. William, 37
Millerites, 37, 55, 65. *See also* Adventists
Ministry, 20, 43, 53, 72, 87
Mother Ann. *See* Lee, Mother Ann
Mother Ann's Work, 35, 42, 84–85. *See also* Spiritualism
Museums, 65, 66, 72, 73, 86, 88
Music. *See* Songs, Singing
Musical instruments, 38, 58, 61, 62, 72
Mount Lebanon, New York, Shaker community at, 79, 87, 88. *See also* New Lebanon, New York, Shaker community at
  Mount Lebanon Shaker Village (museum), 88

National Historic Communal Societies
Association, 77
New England, 2, 10, 28, 30, 59, 60, 87
New Gloucester, Maine, Shaker community
at. *See* Sabbathday Lake, (New
Gloucester), Maine, Shaker community
at
New Harmony, Indiana, 30
New Lebanon, New York
revival at, 9–10, 23
Shaker community at, and church
headquarters (later called Mount
Lebanon), 16, 17, 18, 23, 26, 33, 48,
52, 53, 56, 61
Niskayuna, New York, Shaker community
at (later called Watervliet), 7, 9, 10, 14,
18, 69, 71
North Union, Ohio, Shaker community at,
27, 37
Noyes, John Humphrey, 55. *See also* Oneida
Community
Numbers, of Shakers, 2, 47, 66
Nutter, Ruth, 82

Obedience and discipline, 16, 20, 89
Ohio, 25, 37, 54
Oneida Community, 55
Owen, Robert, 30

Pacifism, 2, 7, 11, 14, 47, 53, 54, 65
international peace conference, 61–62
Patterson, Dr. Daniel, 84–85
Perfectionism, 2, 29, 58, 59–60, 65
Persecution of Shakers, 5, 13–14, 16, 28, 88
arrested for treason and released, 11
Pleasant Hill, Kentucky, Shakertown at, 27,
86
Principles, *ii*, 2, 10, 23, 56, 87. *See also*
Celibacy, Confession of sin, Equality,
Pacifism, Shakerism, Simplicity

Quakers, 4, 7, 70, 71
Shaking Quakers, 4

Recreation, 22, 29, 35–36, 38–39, 46, 50
Religious dissent, 4, 70, 71
Revivals, 9–10, 23, 25, 26, 27, 71
Revolutionary War, 9, 11, 14, 23, 31, 54,
69
Rochester rappings, 44. *See also* Fox sisters,
Spiritualism

Sabbathday Lake (New Gloucester), Maine,
Shaker community at, 18, 62–63,
64–65, 72, 73, 86–87
"Chosen Land," 78
conferences at, 80–82
community life, 1980s, 78, *80–81*, 82–84,
89
Salvation, *xi*, 9, 38, 88
Schwartz, Hillel, 71
Second Coming of Christ, 4, 9, 10, 37, 65
Seeds, 36, 52
Separation of sexes, 17, 20–21, 28
Sex, 5, 15, 47
Shaking, *xi*, 4, 31, 47
Shakerism, *ii*, 1, 10, 30, 47, 56, 64, 66, 71,
72, 76, 78, 84
Shaker Library, at Sabbathday Lake, 70, 79
Shaker Messenger, The, 85
Shaker press, 54
Shaker Quarterly, The, 65, 79
"Shakers, The," 89–90
Shaker Spiritual, The, 84
Shaker Your Plate, 82
Shays' Rebellion, 16
Shirley, Massachusetts, Shaker community
at, 18
"Simple Gifts," *32*, 33, 78
Simplicity, 2, *33*, 33, 35, 40, 52, 66, 86
Sin, 9, 10, 15, 45, 47, 50
Singing, 3, 6, 14, 31, 44, 46, 78, 79, 89
Singing or union meeting, 46, *46*
Smith, Brother Wayne, *80–81*, 82, 89
Social reformers, 29–30, 55–56
Society of Brothers (Bruderhof), 61
Songs, 10, 33, 34, 35, 40, 48, 53, 61, 66,
84–85
musical notation, *32*, 40

Soule, Eldress Gertrude, 62, 73, 75
South Union, Kentucky, Shakertown at,
    26–27, 27, 54, 86
Spiritualism, 34–44, 56, 60
Sprigg, June, 87
Stanley (Standerin), Abraham, 5, 7
Stanton, Edwin, 55
Starbuck, David, 77
Sufism, 88
Swedenborg, Emanuel, 71

*Testimonies of the Life, Character,
    Revelations and Doctrines* (1816), 8–9,
    89
Thompson, Bud, 73
Tolstoy, Count Leo, 53, 56
Traits, Shaker, 29, 36, 53, 59
Tree of Life, 41, 42, 70
Tucker, Brother Micajah, 77
Tyringham, Massachusetts, Shaker
    community at, 18

United Society of Believers, 2, 17, 30, 31,
    43–44, 53. *See also* Believers in Christ's
    Second Appearing
University of Southern Maine, 79
Union Village, Ohio, Shaker community at,
    27
United States government, 54, 56
Utopian communities, 1, 30, 53. *See also*
    Communitarianism

Visions, 40
    of Mother Ann, 3–4, 5, 6, 12, 15, 35
    of Father Joseph, 22
    of Father James Whittaker, 41

Visitors, 31, 33, 37, 55

War of 1812, 54
Wardley, James and Jane, 4, 70, 71
Watervliet, New York (formerly Niskayuna),
    Shaker community at, 34, 37
Watervliet, Ohio, Shaker community at, 27
Wells, Mildred, 76
Wesley, John 71
Western Shaker communities, 23–29, 54,
    60, 86
Whitcher, Benjamin, 20
Whitefield, George, 71
Whittaker, Father James, 5, 16–17, 41
Whitewater, Ohio, Shaker community at,
    27
"Winter Shakers," 47. *See also* Apostates
Witchcraft, 5, 9, 11
Withdrawal from world, 16, 17, 20, 23, 29,
    79
Women, 2, 4, 17, 41, 46, 47, 58–59
Women's rights, 2, 47, 88
Work, 2, 21–22, 24, 28, 29, 48, 59, 73, 79
"World's People," 22, 31, 34, 36, 44, 55,
    57, 63, 65, 86
Worley, Malcolm, 25
Worship, Shaker, 3, 6, *12–13*, 17, 21, 22,
    33, 34, 35, *36*, 44, *45*, 45, 61, 62–63,
    66, 69, 76, 78, 79, 85, 88, 89–91
Worster, Brother Abijah, 60, 69, 70
Wright, Mother Lucy, 17, 22, 23

Youngs, Benjamin Seth, 25
"Youth's Guide in Zion," 50